HOW TO BUILD YOUR
LIONEL® LAYOUT

BY STANLEY W. TRZONIEC

GREENBERG BOOKS

A Division of Kalmbach Publishing Co.

ACKNOWLEDGMENTS

No book of this type is ever the work of one person alone. While the list of acknowledgments is short, the people involved helped more than I ever expected.

My thanks to Sherrie A. Weitzman of Lionel Trains, Inc., who helped answer all my questions and supplied current illustrations of Lionel products. Dick Christianson, Assistant Publisher of *Classic Toy Trains,* helped in numerous ways to strengthen the book with his thoughts and photos from his file. Special thanks to Allan Miller of Greenberg Books, without whose insight this dream of mine would never have become a reality. I also want to acknowledge the help that my wife, Inge, provided. I appreciate her patience, concern, and sympathetic listening.

— Stanley Trzoniec

Editor: Russ Larson
Art director and designer: Sabine Beaupré
Copy editor: Mary Algozin

First Edition, Fourth Printing, 1999

Library of Congress Cataloging-in-Publication Data

Trzoniec, Stanley W.
    How to build your first Lionel layout / by Stanley W. Trzoniec. --
1st ed.
        p.   cm.
    Includes index.
    ISBN 0-89778-393-X
    1. Railroads--Models. 2. Lionel Corporation. I. Title.
TF197.T76 1994   93-36908
625.1'9--dc20   CIP

CONTENTS

There's something about toy trains that has captured the imaginations of thousands and thousands of youngsters and adults since the middle of the last century. And Lionel electric trains, in particular, have fascinated toy train lovers for nearly a hundred years. Is it the red and green lights of the track switches? Is it the man in the milk car who tosses the little milk cans onto— and off of—the platform? Or maybe it's the clicking of metal wheels along metal rails or the smell of ozone from the tiny electric motor? Whatever the source of our fascination, it's real, and toy trains have brought joy to generations of parents and children.

Now it's your turn. The fact that you've bought this book suggests you're interested in getting the trains up off the floor or out from under the Christmas tree. You're ready to become a model railroader.

Just what is model railroading? It's a hobby made up of many hobbies: carpentry, electronics, history, art, and others. This book is designed to introduce you to each of those aspects of the hobby. Author Stan Trzoniec created a small layout ideal for your first exposure to the hobby. As he built it, he photographed it in crisp, clear detail (he's a professional photographer). Then he wrote explanatory text, drawing information from his own background and from other sources as well to provide clear, step-by-step instructions.

As you work your way through the project, you'll find that the demands in each phase of construction are small, and where things may get just a little complicated, the author leads you along so that you don't go astray.

Once you start building your layout, you'll find it's all pretty easy. Before long you'll be throwing switches with the best of 'em. Your trains will be rolling flawlessly over rail joints, around curves, and into sidings.

But this is only the beginning. Once you've mastered the principles and techniques the author has outlined here, you'll be ready to try new techniques, plan your own layout, and build your own toy train empire!

That, in fact, is the motivation behind this book. The author, a toy train enthusiast himself, wants you to share in the fun of the world's greatest hobby—model railroading with toy trains! You're gonna love it.

Dick Christianson
Assistant Publisher
Classic Toy Trains Magazine

The Devil surely took possession of me that fine post-Christmas afternoon in 1947. I cranked up the throttle on the transformer of my new Lionel train set, and my train took off at top speed. As the train went into that first curve, my new no. 2025 steam locomotive flew off that 27" diameter curve and rolled right into the nativity scene my father had set up under the Christmas tree. Moving like a flash, I peeled the cotton off the side rods and drivers to hide my evil deed and to get things back to normal before the master of the house came forth to see why it was suddenly quiet.

The Christmas I received my first Lionel train set was special. But that was only the beginning. The next Christmas season I spent many hours with my nose pressed against the window at Bamberger's department store in Newark, looking at the huge Lionel display and dreaming about adding all those magical trains and accessories to my setup. Soon my dreams began to come true.

Every year my trains were set up from Thanksgiving until New Year's. And every Christmas I received gifts for my layout. First the buildings of Plasticville, then the Lionel milk car, cattle car, and even that funny-looking coal car. Single main lines turned into double-tracked lines with trains highballing around the basement. I remember the sounds of that famous whistle, the smoke, and—oh yes—the smell.

Each year my wish list taken from those beautifully illustrated Lionel catalogs was evenly distributed among the relatives. Uncle Johnny always called (secretly of course) and asked me what I wanted for my trains. He just knew it was better to receive something you *really* wanted than socks or underwear. My father, on the other hand, always appeared with that right accessory every year as if he was a mind reader. (Gee, my kids say the same thing of me now!)

Special times during those childhood years were when we turned all the overhead lights off and the trains ran through the villages in the semidarkness with engines smoking, horns and whistles blaring, and lights piercing the darkness.

Those childhood years passed all too quickly, and over time my Lionel equipment was misplaced, given away, or sold—with the exception of my first locomotive. Through some miracle old no. 2025 is still with me.

Stan Trzoniec and his sister pose by his Lionel layout sometime in the very late 1940s.

As an adult, my interest in Lionel trains was rekindled. I reacquired the accessories I had as a boy and even enlarged my collection by visiting train shows and buying collections. Soon I plan to build my dream layout, which will be a variation of Lionel's famous 1949 New York display.

If you've just discovered Lionel trains, you have many pleasurable times ahead. Great new products keep flowing from Lionel Trains, Inc. The modern Lionel train enthusiast has so much to buy and use, it almost staggers the imagination. New diesel engines with finer details, big steam engines, complete sets, and a wide variety of cars and accessories are all available. All you have to do is go to your dealer and have a look. And don't forget to take your son or daughter along. Part of the enjoyment of toy trains is being together and sharing.

But just how do you begin? Well that's what this book is all about. I'm going to show you how to build a small Lionel 4' x 8' layout in step-by-step fashion. I also want to stir your imagination and get you dreaming about bigger and better layouts. So sit back, flip through the pages, and make a list of what you'll need to build that first layout—but most of all, dream. That's the key. Soon your dreams will become reality. And that's when the fun really starts.

Stanley W. Trzoniec

CHAPTER ONE

Lionel Electric Trains: An American Tradition

Fig. 1-1. The man who started it all—Joshua Lionel Cowen. The Lionel Corporation, starting as a small shop in New York in 1901, grew to be the biggest model train maker in the world in the late 1940s. Photo courtesy of Lionel Trains, Inc.

Fig. 1-2. As this ad from the 1950s suggests, a Lionel train set made a wonderful Christmas present then and still does today. For many people trains and Christmas just seem to go together.

This book is about building a small O gauge Lionel layout complete with scenery, buildings, and some operating accessories. Just the fact that you've picked up this book implies that you know something about Lionel electric trains. Perhaps you had a Lionel train set as a child, and now you want to build a Lionel layout for yourself or your son or daughter (or grandchild). Or maybe you always wanted a Lionel train set when you were a child, but weren't fortunate enough to get one. Now you can buy one for yourself and create your dream empire.

Another possibility is that you've heard of Lionel trains and want to see just what the excitement is all about. Lionel is one of this country's most recognizable brand names. That's partly because the name has been around a long time—since 1901—and partly because of the marketing that the firm did during its heyday.

THE PLAN

Many people consider the company's founder, Joshua Lionel Cowen, fig. 1-1, to have been a marketing genius. True, his company produced quality products—but it was the marketing plan that created the demand. I think it's safe to say that during the decade following World War II most boys in America wanted a Lionel electric train for Christmas. See fig. 1-2. I know I did, and I was lucky enough to get one. A Lionel train set is still a popular Christmas gift.

Catalogs. One of Lionel's main marketing tools was the beautiful color catalogs (fig. 1-3) they produced each year. There were always new trains and accessories to dream about.

Display layouts. When I was a boy the Christmas selling season didn't begin until after Thanksgiving. I remember how the Thanksgiving Day parade always concluded with Santa on the last float. That signaled the beginning of the Christmas season, and I knew I'd be able to visit those great department store Lionel displays soon. See fig. 1-4. It was hard for any kid to come away from one of those displays without wanting something like it for himself.

Advertising. Lionel's consumer ads were cleverly done. Some stressed the father-son relationship, as demonstrated in fig. 1-5. Others were directed at the boys and told them how they could be the engineer of electric trains that were just

Fig. 1-3. When it came to Lionel trains, nothing compared to the annual "wish books" published by the company in the 1940s and 1950s. Millions were printed. Young engineers would peruse this catalog and then place an order with Dad for their yearly gift of trains.

Fig. 1-4. Display layouts like this, operating in department stores and hobby shops every Christmas season, were an important part of Lionel's marketing efforts. Children and adults loved to visit a favorite store to see the latest Lionel trains and accessories in operation.

like the real ones. See fig. 1-6. The entire program—catalogs, display layouts, and ads—made Lionel trains a household word and the gift every boy wanted to have in the late 1940s and early 1950s.

Quality products. No amount of marketing genius can sustain a company if the products are not of good quality and appreciated by the consumer. Lionel produced quality products that were easy to use. Lionel decided to use a three-rail track system early on and stuck with it. It has proved to be a reliable system that is easy to wire. The locomotives, cars, and accessories were made to last. The fact that there is so much good used Lionel equipment today is testimony to the quality built in by the factory.

THE ERAS

Collectors of Lionel trains have defined three major eras of Lionel manufacture: prewar, postwar and modern era.

Prewar. In the early days, Lionel made a line of trains bigger than O gauge. They were called Standard gauge trains and had a track spacing, or gauge, of $2\frac{1}{8}$" between the rails. O gauge trains, the subject of this book, weren't introduced until the early 1930s. With their $1\frac{1}{4}$" track gauge and much tighter curves, these smaller trains were more practical to set up in the average home. As the country came out of the Great Depression, sales of Lionel O gauge trains really began to take off. This period of Lionel's history ended in 1942, when train production was suspended so the factory could be used to produce goods needed for the war effort.

Postwar. This era began in 1945. Lionel managed to produce a catalog for the 1945 Christmas season with an offering of one train set. Production quickly resumed in 1946. The company's best years followed the war. This was the time when the O gauge electric train reached its peak popularity. By the late 1950s, electric trains began to feel heavy competition from other toys, many of them quite inexpensive, and sales began to fall off. In 1959, Cowen, then 82 years old, sold

Fig. 1-5. Some of Lionel's ads targeted fathers and stressed how the father-son relationship would be strengthened by building a Lionel layout together.

Fig 1-6. Other Lionel ads, like this one, were directed at boys. A boy could imagine he was the engineer and operate his trains just like the real thing!

his interest in the company to his nephew. The decline of sales continued until production ceased in 1969. So the postwar era extended from 1945 to 1969.

Modern era. In 1970 General Mills bought the Lionel brand name and tooling and made Lionel a part of its Model Products Corporation, a subsidiary. MPC had some success with Lionel, but a 1983 move of production to Mexico proved to be a disaster. Production was moved back to Michigan in 1985. Shortly thereafter the name and tooling were sold to Richard Kughn, an entrepreneur and Lionel collector, who formed a new company called Lionel Trains, Inc. Since then LTI has reestablished the original reputation for quality. The company has reintroduced many old-time favorites and offered many new products.

GETTING STARTED WITH LIONEL TRAINS

Visit a hobby shop. Before purchasing anything, I suggest you visit a hobby shop that has a good selection of Lionel trains, such as the one shown in fig. 1-7. On that first visit, just browse and get an idea of what's available. Pick up a new catalog and ask questions. If you want to start on a serious note, don't go to a store around the busiest part of the Christmas holidays because you'll get the least amount of attention. As a merchant myself, selling Lionel throughout the year, I can offer this advice: Two of the best times to visit a hobby shop are early on a Saturday morning before the customers start to file in and during a weekday. It might even

be worth taking a few hours off work to be able to spend some uninterrupted time with a knowledgeable hobby shop owner or manager.

The question of where to buy Lionel trains has come up many, many times. Some folks like the convenience of discount chains; others like the small talk, information, and service available at full-service train shops. Discount chains employ people who serve in many departments, and if trains are not their strong suit, they almost can't wait to get you rung up and out the door.

Train and hobby shops, on the other hand, have a vested interest in your well-being. If you buy a train set now, you will come back later for more cars, engines, track, and accessories. In a full-service shop you get advice on what is the best engine, car, or accessory for your interests, and your train-related problems can be solved by people who have a genuine interest in the hobby and want to see it grow. Surprisingly enough, the price difference between a discount store and a hobby shop is not that great. You certainly have a choice here—but for the long term, I'd recommend the full-service hobby shop.

Visit a train show. Model train shows, fig. 1-8, are held frequently in most major cities across the country. Your local hobby shop is a good place to find out when and where the shows are in your area. You can also check the listings in magazines such as *Classic Toy Trains* or *Model Railroader*.

At a show you'll be able to see portable or modular Lionel layouts in operation and talk to

1-7. The author recommends visiting a hobby shop to see what's available and to get answers to your questions about the hobby. He also recommends making your purchases there because they service what they sell.

the hobbyists who have built them. You'll also be able to see the variety of used Lionel equipment that's for sale and get an idea of the going prices.

Determine the scope of your involvement. After you have a better idea of what this hobby entails, give some thought to how involved you want to become. Will you want just a loop of track set up under the Christmas tree once a year, or are you willing to take the plunge and dedicate energy, time, and space in your home to the project?

The layout I'll show you how to build in this book, fig. 1-9, will take you from the loop of track on the floor to a miniature empire, complete with scenery and buildings. It's

Fig. 1-8. Visiting a train show like this Greenberg Great Train, Dollhouse & Toy Show in Philadelphia will give you a good idea of what's available in the used Lionel market. You'll also get to see some portable or modular Lionel layouts in operation.

Fig. 1-9. Overall view of the 4' x 8' Lionel layout that the author describes how to build, starting in Chapter III.

something you can sink your teeth into without spending a great deal of time or money. A 4' x 8' layout won't take up much space in your home. And for those of you who plan to have it up only during the holiday season, I'll describe how you can design the layout so it can be taken apart and stored.

The purpose of this book is to help you get started and, I hope, keep you in the hobby for years.

SCALE VS HI-RAIL

Lionel trains and their counterparts—like K-Line, Williams, Weaver, and others—that run on standard three-rail track are known in the trade as "hi-rail" or "tinplate." The former term refers to the height of the larger O gauge track, the latter to the time when toy trains were simply stamped out of tinplated steel.

You'll hear the term "scale" used when you're in a hobby shop. This refers to model railroading where the hobbyist builds models that closely depict the real thing. An O scale model is 1:48 the size of the real train; $1/4"$ on the model equals a foot on the real train—exactly. These trains run on two-rail track, like real railroads, and they usually have more realistic details. Other popular scales are HO (1:87) and N (1:160).

What's best, scale or hi-rail? If you're a nitpicker, scale models would probably appeal to you more. If you're into family fun, Lionel trains and their counterparts are the way to go.

SELECTING EQUIPMENT

Train sets. Lionel sets usually have a minimum of a loco-

Fig. 1-10. Purchasing a Lionel train set is a good way to start. A set like this one contains a locomotive, cars, track, a transformer, and sometimes a few other items. It's all in one package, and the price is less than if you purchased the items individually.

Fig. 1-11. If you're interested in steam locomotives, Lionel has some beauties like this 2-8-4 (2 pilot wheels, 8 driving wheels, 4 trailing wheels) lettered for Pere Marquette no. 1201.

motive, three or four cars, and a caboose. In addition, in the box you'll find enough track to make a decent size oval; a transformer; a lockon, which is a connector to get power from the transformer to the track; and wire to accomplish this feat. A typical set is shown in fig. 1-10. There's everything you need to get up and running with a minimum effort on your part. This is the very best way to get going. It not only allows you the convenience of having everything in one package, but the savings are also impressive. As a hobby shop owner I can tell you that if you bought everything contained in a train set individually, the total price would be much higher. And if you buy sets during the months before Christmas, you'll usually find them on sale.

Steam vs. diesels. Probably one of the first things you are going to notice is that the sets come with either steam or diesel locomotives. How do you decide which to select? For starters, steam locomotives, fig. 1-11, offer some additional features children (and adults) find fascinating. There's the action of the siderods, the smoking stack, and the front headlight. Steam relates to the golden age of railroading in this country, and this is a plus for history buffs. For action, they're simply hard to beat.

Diesel locomotives, on the other hand, are just plain colorful. The red, yellow and silver markings of the famed Santa Fe "Warbonnet" paint scheme, for instance, caught the attention of young folks when this engine was first issued over forty years ago. The Erie Lackawanna PA-2 shown in fig. 1-12 is a beautiful paint scheme too. Now you can choose from the color schemes used by many different railroads, since Lionel keeps adding new models each year.

My advice is to go with your gut feelings when deciding between steam and diesel. Remember that no matter what the initial choice is, you can always add other motive power later on to balance your railroad's needs.

Freight cars. You're going to need some freight cars to generate business for your railroad. The most common one is the boxcar (fig. 1-13), which is

Fig. 1-12. If you like diesels, many colorful models are offered, like this nice Erie Lackawanna scheme on an Alco PA-2.

1-13. Boxcars are a common type of car used by railroads to haul a wide variety of goods. This "Goofy" car is a special collector's edition. Normally boxcars are lettered for prototype railroads.

nothing more than a box with wheels attached. These cars are important revenue producers for any railroad. In this grouping, called house cars, you'll find refrigerator cars for produce, automobile cars, fig. 1-14, and stock cars for the transportation of cattle and similar livestock.

Gondolas are low-sided and are used for hauling heavy loads like steel beams, scrap metal, and other commodities. Hopper cars, fig. 1-15, are used for hauling bulk commodities like coal and grain. The contents of the hopper cars are unloaded through doors under the car by gravity.

Flatcars, fig. 1-16, are very common. We see them in service carrying long pipes, lumber, truck trailers ("piggyback" service), and containers. See figs. 1-17 and 1-18. Tank cars, fig. 1-19, are used to haul oil, chemicals, and other liquids.

1-14. To protect new automobiles from vandalism, they are carried in covered cars like this Grand Trunk (GT) in the center. The automobiles are loaded from the ends.

1-15. Open hoppers like this are commonly used today to transport coal to power plants.

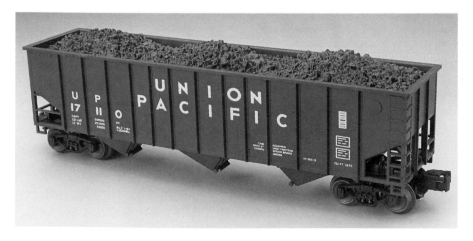

Fig. 1-16. There are many types of flatcars. This one with bulkheads is used to ship pulpwood.

Fig. 1-17. Right, center: Many truck trailers travel most of the way by train on special flatcars like this.

1-18. Other special cars are just for hauling containers. These can handle double-stacked containers.

Lionel makes all of these prototype freight cars. In addition, the company offers a selection of non-prototypical cars that are simply fun to operate, like searchlight cars (fig. 1-20) and side-dump lumber and coal cars.

Last, and certainly not to be forgotten, is the caboose, fig. 1-21, that brings up the rear of the train (except for modern freight trains, where they've been mostly eliminated).

Passenger cars. Even though traveling by train isn't

Fig. 1-19. Tank cars come in many sizes and are used to haul fuel, chemicals, and other liquids.

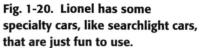

as popular as it once was, we still have Amtrak passenger service in this country. And it's really a nice way to travel. Prior to 1971, all major railroads operated their own passenger trains.

Lionel produces beautiful, long aluminum passenger cars painted and lettered for Amtrak and other railroads. See fig. 1-22. If you're modeling an older era, you can use heavyweight cars, more commonly called "Madison" cars. Behind a vintage steam engine they are hard to beat—especially when the room lights are turned down and all those tiny people appear through lighted coach windows.

I hope my suggestions and the basic information presented in this chapter will help you get started on your way to a lifelong interest in Lionel trains.

1-21. Don't forget the caboose. Up until the mid-1980s almost all freight trains had a caboose at the rear. Most modern trains don't use them.

Fig. 1-22. Operating passenger trains is another option to consider. Lionel offers equipment lettered for a number of railroads, including this colorful Santa Fe passenger train set.

CHAPTER TWO

Basics of Track and Track Planning

Fig. 2-1. One of the first decisions you'll have to make is what type of track you'll use to build your layout, O27 or O gauge. The author chose O gauge track to build this 4' x 8' layout, and he explains why he prefers O gauge.

Now that you know a bit about the basics of Lionel trains, you probably want to set up a simple oval of track and get some trains running. If you've already bought a train set, I'd recommend you do that right away. If you haven't purchased anything yet, let me explain the two different types of track and equip-ment offered by Lionel—O27 and O gauge.

O27 VS O GAUGE

This can be a confusing sub-ject for a beginner. O27 origi-nally was the term used to de-scribe curved track that would form a 27" diameter circle. Li-onel still offers that diameter track and uses it in most of its train sets. With O gauge track, the smallest diameter circle you can make is 31". Is that pretty clear for starters?

Cross section. The differ-ences between O27 and O go beyond the diameter of the cir-cles made by the curved track sections. Although O27 and O have the same gauge (1¼" be-tween the outer rails), the rail

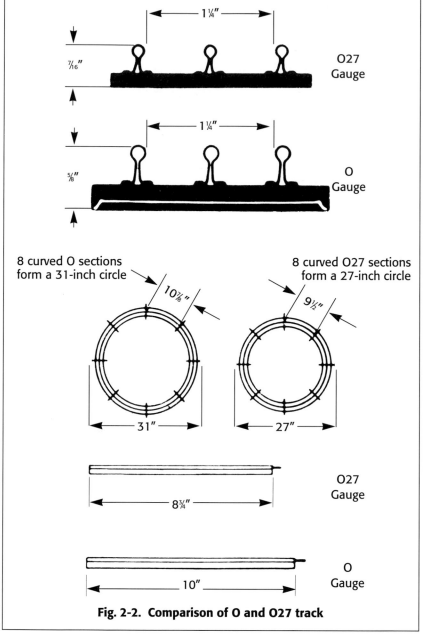

Fig. 2-2. Comparison of O and O27 track

height and cross section are different, as shown in fig. 2-2. Including ties, O27 track has a height of about $7/16$" with a rail height of $1/4$". Lionel O gauge measures $5/8$" high with ties, with a $3/8$" track height. For practical purposes the two track lines are not easily compatible. It's difficult to join a piece of O27 track to a piece of O gauge track.

Wide-radius curves. To further complicate the subject, Lionel now offers two additional types of "wide-radius" curved track with the O27 track profile. So you can buy O27 curved track that forms 27", 42", or 54" diameter circles. The latter two are described as "O27 wide-radius O42" and "O27 wide-radius O54," respectively.

In O gauge you can also buy curved track that forms either 54" or 72" diameter circles. That track is simply designated O54 and O72. Lionel's regular O gauge track forms a 31" diameter circle, O54 a 54" diameter circle, and O72 a 72" diameter circle. See fig. 2-3. Are you still with me?

O27 equipment. Lionel train sets contain O27 track as a part of the package. Engines

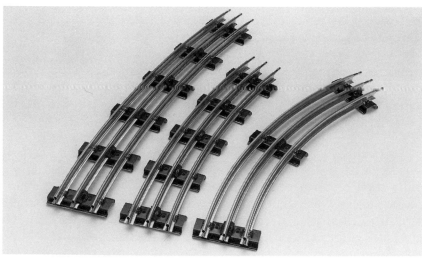

Fig. 2-3. As you expand your layout, you may want to get into larger-radius curves. From right to left in O gauge are O31, O54 and O72 curves.

Fig. 2-4. Here's a comparison of an O gauge boxcar with an O27 boxcar. O27 equipment is smaller so it can more easily negotiate the sharper curves.

and cars that come with the sets are short in length (fig. 2-4) to negotiate the tighter 27" diameter curves. If later you purchase longer, more scale-sized O gauge engines, freight cars, and passenger cars (which you will), you are going to have a problem running them on the tighter O27 curves and through O27 switches. You can stick with O27 and go with wide-radius curves to operate this longer equipment, but O27 switches will still pose a problem. Using O gauge track and switches from the start will help you avoid these problems.

Which track is best? When you visit a hobby shop you may hear a lot of talk concerning the use of O27 or O gauge track as the standard

Fig. 2-5. LIONEL O GAUGE TRACK AND SWITCHES		
12840	Insulated Track	Used to activate most Lionel operating accessories. 10" long.
65500	Straight Track	Each section is 10" long.
65505	½ Straight Track	Each section is 5½" long.
65523	40" Extra Long Straight	Equal to four sections of regular O Gauge straight track.
65501	Curved Track	Eight sections will create 31" diameter circle. 11¹⁄₁₆" long.
65504	½ Curved Track	Each section is 6⅛" long.
5554	O54 Wide-Radius Curved	Sixteen sections will create 54" diameter circle. 10¾" long.
5572	O72 Wide-Radius Curved	Sixteen sections will create 72" diameter circle. 14⅛" long.
5540	90-degree Crossover	Used for building figure-eight layouts. 8⁵⁄₁₆" long.
5545	45-degree Crossover	Used for elongated figure-eight layouts. 11¾" long.
5543	Insulating Pins	Used to replace steel pins in creating insulated sections.
5551	Steel Pins	Used to join track sections. Three per section are required.
5530	Remote Uncoupler	Uncouples cars; activates operating cars by remote control.
12743	O Gauge Track Clips	Secures track on temporary layouts. 12 per package.
62900	Lockon	Used to attach wires to track for electrical connections.
62905	Lockon & Wires	Same as above, but includes lengths of wire for connections.

O GAUGE REMOTE CONTROL SWITCHES

Create interesting O Gauge track layout designs with the added convenience of remote control operation. These switches are designed so that the motor can be placed on either side of the switch. Switch has a lighted controller and switch lamp, and a direct power capability so it may be connected directly to transformer power. Straight track on each O Gauge switch is 10" long; curved track section is 11¹⁄₁₆" long. Straight track on each O72 switch is 14¼" long; curved track section is 14⅛" long.

5132	O Remote Switch (Right)	For remote control train entry into sidings, passing tracks, etc.
5133	O Remote Switch (Left)	Same as above, but left-hand turnout section.
5165	O72 Remote Switch (Right)	Wide-radius remote control switch for sidings, etc.
5166	O72 Remote Switch (Left)	Same as above, but left-hand turnout section.

Fig. 2-6. LIONEL O27 GAUGE TRACK AND SWITCHES

12841	Insulated Track	Used to activate most Lionel operating accessories. 8¾" long.
65038	Straight Track	Each section is 8¾" long.
65019	½ Straight Track	Each section is 4¹³⁄₁₆" long.
65017	Straight Track	Four sections O27 straight track. Each Section 8¾" long.
65024	Extra Long Straight Track	Equal to four sections of regular O27 straight track. 35" long.
65033	Curved Track	Eight sections will create 27" diameter circle. 9⅝" long.
65014	½ Curved Track	Each section is 5⁷⁄₁₆" long.
5012	Curved Track (4 ea.)	Four sections will form half of a 27" diameter circle. 9⅝" long.
5049	O42 Wide-Radius Curved	Twelve sections will create 42" diameter circle. 10⅞" long.
5113	O54 Wide-Radius Curved	Sixteen sections will create 54" diameter circle. 14½" long.
5020	90-degree Crossover	Used for building figure-eight layouts. 7⅞" long.
5023	45-degree Crossover	Used for elongated figure-eight layouts. 9⁵⁄₁₆" long.
5041	Insulating Pins	Used to replace steel pins in creating insulated sections.
5042	Steel Pins	Used to join track sections. Three per section required.
5149	Remote Uncoupler	Uncouples cars; activates operating cars by remote control.
12746	Remote Uncoupling Track	Allows O Gauge operating cars to be activated on O27 layouts.
62901	O27 Track Clips	Secures track on temporary layouts. 12 per box.
62900	Lockon	Used to attach wires to track for electrical connections.
62905	Lockon & Wires	Same as above, but includes lengths of wire for connections.

O27 MANUAL AND REMOTE CONTROL SWITCHES

Create interesting O27 Gauge track layout designs with either manual or remote control operation. Straight track on each O27 Gauge switch is 8¾" long; curved track section is 9⅝" long. Straight track on each O42 switch is 13⅜" long; curved track section is 10⁵⁄₁₆" long.

5022	O27 Manual Switch (Right)	Economy switching with hand-throw lever on switch.
5021	O27 Manual Switch (Left)	Same as above, but left-hand manual operation.
5122	O27 Remote Switch (Right)	For remote control train entry into sidings, passing tracks, etc.
5121	O27 Remote Switch (Left)	Same as above, but left-hand turnout section.
5168	O42 Remote Switch (Right)	Wide-radius remote control switch for sidings, etc.
5167	O42 Remote Switch (Left)	Same as above, but left-hand turnout section.

for your layout. Since all of this is subjective, I guess the final decision rests with you and your future hobby plans.

My recommendation is to go with O gauge track for your layout and keep the O27 for your annual setup around the Christmas tree. It will be easier to expand an O gauge layout because this gauge offers a more versatile assortment of track, switches, and other components, including the wider-radius O72 curves. Also, O gauge track is more rugged; the switch motors can be moved from side to side to accommodate differences in track plans; and for larger layouts the longer cars just look better when operating around those wider curves.

I personally prefer O gauge even for a small layout, and that's what I suggest using for the 4' x 8' layout we'll begin building in the next chapter.

The accompanying charts, figs. 2-5 and 2-6, show the line of track available from Lionel in both O and O27.

STRAIGHT TRACK

Straight track. For O gauge, the standard track length is 10"; for O27, it's 8¾" (fig. 2-2). Extra-long pieces, which are four times the standard, are offered in each track line. On a large layout it's a good idea to use as many of these long pieces as you can to reduce the number of rail joints. Each rail joint presents a potential for future electrical and mechanical problems, so the fewer you have the better off you'll be.

Half straight track. Half sections (fig. 2-7) come in handy in tight spots and for sidings where an extra full-length section just won't fit.

Cutting track. Sometimes you're going to want a length of track different from what's offered. You can cut the track fairly easily to any desired length. First, using a pair of nippers, remove the pins from the end you'll be discarding by rocking the pin outward. Then chuck one rail in a vise at a time and cut the rail with a fine hacksaw or model saw. Replace the track pins and you now have a track section of the length you require.

TRACK SWITCHES

Basics. Switches seem to concern beginning operators, so let's try to simplify things. Switches, more properly called turnouts among prototype railroaders and scale model-ers, divert trains from one route to another, much as you do when you turn your auto-mobile onto one street or an-other. Since trains depend on rails, they need mechanical devices to route themselves. Switches take care of this job. Regardless of whether you are working in O27 or O gauge, switches come in right- or left-hand types. With a right-hand switch, the curved part of the switch goes to the right; on a left-hand switch, to the left, as shown in fig. 2-8. The curved section of each switch matches

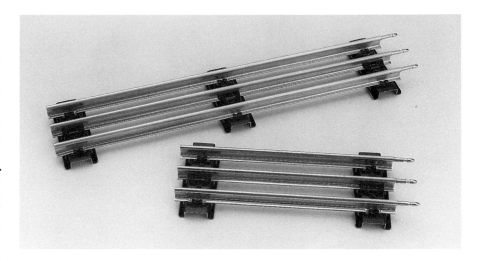

Fig. 2-7. Shown above are a full O gauge straight track section and a half section. If you plan cleverly, you can use half sections and eliminate the need for cutting track.

Fig. 2-8. To route trains, you need switches. This is a pair of O27 switch-es. The bottom one is manual, the top operates electrically.

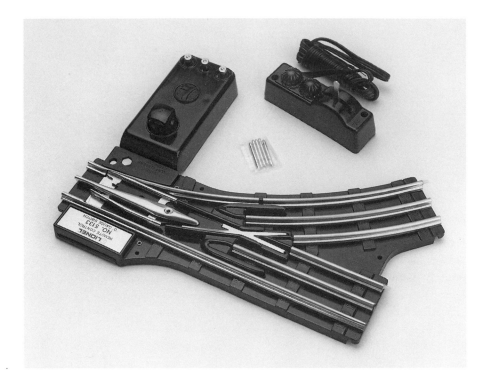

Fig. 2-9. Shown here is Lionel's top-of-the-line O gauge switch with a built-in 31" diameter curve. Track pins are included as well as a lighted controller showing the track alignment position of the switch.

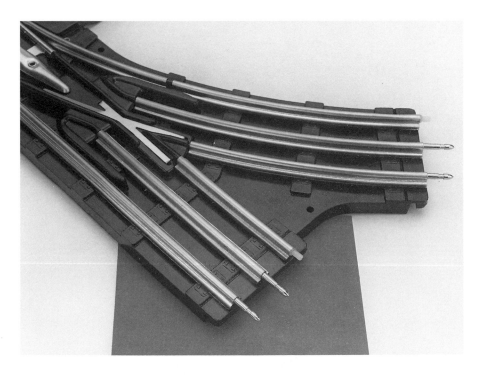

Fig. 2-10. The "non-derailing" feature built into all Lionel electric switches is triggered by a factory-installed insulated pin positioned as shown. If the switch is in the wrong position as the train approaches, it changes automatically; you don't have to worry about the engine and cars derailing.

the exact radius of the curved sectional track types (fig. 2-9).

Non-derailing feature. Internally the switches have an innovative design feature that takes some of the frustration out of operating trains. When the non-derailing feature senses that a train is approaching a switch thrown against it (one set for the opposite direction), it automatically throws the switch, thereby preventing a derailment. This electrical contact is done through the base of the switch; it doesn't require any manual hookup on your part. All you have to remember is to keep the insulated pins in the positions they come in from the factory, fig. 2-10, and keep the rails clean to provide the necessary electrical contact.

Fixed-voltage plug. Electrically operated O gauge switches can get power from the track or directly to the switch terminals from a separate power source (transformer). If you want to operate the machines from a separate power source, you plug in the fixed-voltage plug that disconnects the track power. See fig. 2-11. On small layouts, operating the switches from track power is okay; but remember that the voltage to the switch mechanism will go up and down depending upon the voltage supplied to the track to make the train go fast or slow. When the train is moving along at a good clip, the track voltage will be high and the switch will snap with moderate enthusiasm. With a slow-moving train the track voltage will be low, and the throwing action of the switch machine will be that much slower.

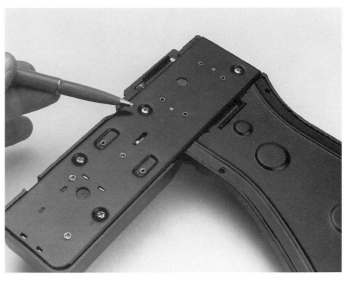

Fig. 2-11. Fixed voltage plugs on O gauge switches are used to draw constant voltage directly from the transformer, rather than variable voltage from the track. This results in consistent and reliable performance.

Fig. 2-12. With O gauge switches, the switch machine can be reversed for tight applications such as in yards, on sidings, or near mountains or tunnels. The two top screws do it all

With a fixed-voltage plug, the switch motor is electrically disconnected from the track and a separate power supply (your transformer's accessory terminals) is applied to the posts, as shown in fig. 2-11. One thing to keep in mind regarding this fixed voltage plug is that if you decide to run your switches by track power alone, you must remove the plug. When it's in place it disconnects the machine from the track power.

Removable switch motors. Another feature of the O gauge no. 5132 and 5133 switches is that you can flop the switch machines. If there isn't room for the machine on one side of your layout, you can move it to the other. Simply remove two screws, switch the part, and replace the screws. See fig. 2-12. There's no hassle and no additional wiring. It's easy! A bundle of information comes with any of the O27 or O gauge switches. Read it, keep it, and refer to it often.

OTHER TRACK TYPES

Remote uncouplers. The next most valuable piece of track that you should consider including on your layout is the remote uncoupling section shown in fig. 2-13. In years past they were called either

Fig. 2-13. To uncouple cars or run certain accessories, an operating uncoupling track section, shown above, is required.

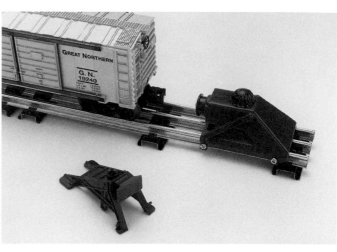

Fig. 2-14. To have trains cross at junctions, Lionel makes both 45 and 90 degree crossovers in both O and O27 gauges.

Fig. 2-15. To keep cars from running off the ends of the track, install bumpers. At the top is the deluxe model, complete with a spring buffer return and light; at bottom is the "manual" type that just clips into the track.

RCS (remote control section) or UCS (uncoupling control section), but today Lionel lists them as remote uncouplers. Regardless of what they're called, they are available in both O27 and O gauge product lines and perform the same way. There is an electromagnet in the center of the track section, which you activate by pressing a controller button. When cars equipped with knuckle couplers are positioned over the magnet, they will uncouple when you push the button. You'll want uncoupling tracks on each industrial spur so you can spot cars at the different industries.

These uncoupling sections are also designed to activate and unload operating cars such as log cars, coal cars, and cattle cars. When an operating car is spotted over an uncoupling track and the unload button is pressed, current is fed to the car's mechanism by means of sliding shoes on the car. The shoes make contact with special control rails on the uncou-

pling section. (There are a total of five rails, and the two inside the running rails are the control rails.)

Like the switches, uncoupling track sections can be operated directly from track power or from a separate supply. Operating them from a separate supply is the preferred method.

Insulated track. Insulated track sections are used to activate some accessories automatically as the train enters the section. Here's how they work. Locomotives pick up current from the center rail and the two outer rails. If one outer rail is insulated from the other outer rail and from adjoining tracks at each end, the locomotive will still run fine. Insulated track sections have one outer rail insulated from the other outer rail and from all adjoining rails.

An accessory (a grade crossing signal, for instance) is connected to the insulated rail with a lockon. As the locomotive travels into this insulated

section, its metal wheels bridge the gap between the live rail and the insulated one, acting as a switch and turning on current to the grade crossing signal. The accessory will operate until the last car passes over the insulated section.

In years past, you had to make your own insulated track sections by insulating an outer rail with thin cardboard (like a matchbook cover) and replacing the metal rail joiners at each end with fiber pins so an electrical gap was created.

Many accessories can also be activated by the trusty 153C connector (no longer being produced, but used ones are easy to find). The connector contains a simple single-pole switch, which is closed by the weight of a passing train. When the switch closes, the accessory is activated. While this is a simple and reliable way to operate accessories, you must leave a few track sections free to float (move up and down freely) in order to allow the switch to work up and down as the train enters and leaves the section of track.

Crossovers. Crossings (fig. 2-14) or crossovers, as Lionel calls them, are offered in both 45 and 90 degree angles for both O27 and O gauge track. They are useful in making very different traffic patterns on your layout.

Bumpers. Adding a bumper, fig. 2-15, is a practical and prototypical way to prevent cars from running off the end of the track on a siding (and maybe rolling off onto the floor). Both unlighted and lighted bumpers are available.

LET'S RUN SOME TRAINS

Floor running. Setting up track on the floor is an easy way to get started, and it can be fun for a while. As you may have already discovered, running a train on a rug leaves a lot to be desired. Even the smallest amount of lubricant on the engine or cars will start to pick up lint and put it in the darndest places, from engine gears to car axles. This will eventually cause serious operating problems.

Operating trains on a wood or linoleum floor is much better, but you'll quickly find that the track starts to separate, especially at the curves, from the movement and weight of the trains themselves. You can check this separation temporarily by using track clips, but it is a short-lived solution at best. Tall accessories and buildings get knocked over by the family cat, and pretty soon you're frustrated.

Plywood platform. A more permanent solution is to mount your track on a plywood platform. While you can just

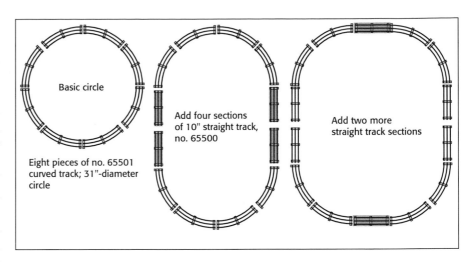

Fig. 2-16. The basic circle of track can be extended in various oval configurations by adding straight pieces to the sides, top, and bottom.

place the plywood on the rug, a much better idea is to mount some 1x4s or 2x4s under the plywood for stability. Now you can screw the track in place, so you won't have to worry about it coming apart. Also, now you have a stable base on which to place buildings, and you won't have to worry about picking up lint from the rug.

Permanent layouts. By far, the best way to enjoy Lionel trains is by building what I call either seasonal or permanent layouts.

Seasonal layouts are the ones that are set up in the basement or spare room for the holidays. They are basically plywood platforms on legs; the added height makes it easier to work on the layout and more fun to watch the trains. If properly designed, a layout of this type can be taken down and stored with relative ease.

You can also design layouts that can fit under a bed, ready to be rolled out when needed. Naturally, tall accessories, buildings, and scenery items have to be removed, but in cramped quarters, this might be the way to go. Another idea

is to design a layout that folds up for storage.

When you become seriously involved in this hobby you'll want a permanent layout, one that you work on and enjoy year around. If you are a beginner, right out front I'm going to tell you that layouts, like people, are highly individual. They come in all shapes and sizes. Some look great, others look good only to the model railroaders who built them. Don't be discouraged if that first layout doesn't make the cover of *Classic Toy Trains* Magazine. As you gain experience, your modeling efforts will begin to look better and better.

I'm going to describe how to build a 4' x 8' layout that will give you a taste of what's involved while limiting your investment of both time and money. I should warn you that building this small Lionel layout may lead to bigger and better layouts as time goes on.

I started by running trains on the floor, then built a 4 x 8, and now have a layout that occupies over 160 square feet of space. I'm now in the process of building a new house, and

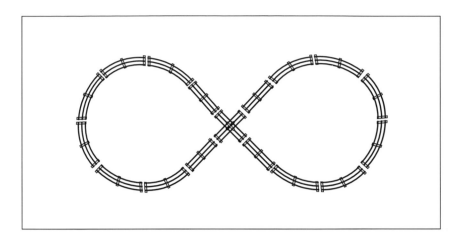

Fig. 2-17 A crossing like this 90 degree one adds variety to train operation.

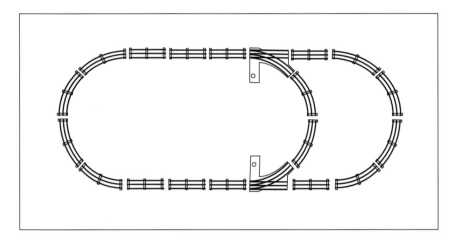

Fig. 2-18. Add a pair of switches and you can vary the route of the train.

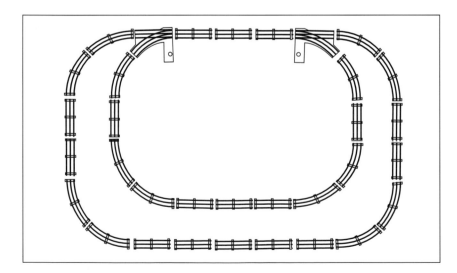

Fig. 2-19. By making the layout more square, you can run one train in the inner or outer loop while the other one remains parked.

I'm looking forward to building a layout that will occupy about 500 square feet!

TRACK ARRANGEMENTS

Before you begin building a permanent layout, I'd suggest you experiment with a variety of track configurations. This experimentation is fun in itself, and it will also give you a better idea of what's practical and what you personally like.

Variations on the oval. Since your train set came with the basic oval, let's start with this configuration and build on it. Fig. 2-16 shows that by adding straight sections you can make the simple oval a little more interesting. The plans shown use O gauge track, but you can build similar plans with O27.

Adding a crossing. Probably the most inexpensive way to break up the dizzying effect of trains running around in a circle is to insert a simple 90 degree crossing, as shown in figure 2-17. In this way at least your trains run first one way, then the other. In either O27 or O gauge, this figure eight can easily fit on a 4' x 8' sheet of plywood and still have room left over for some simple scenery, buildings, or an industry or two.

Another idea is to use the Lionel graduated trestle set and run a train up and over itself. A little imagination goes a long way here.

Adding some switches. Purchase one right- and one left-hand switch, and you can design some really interesting plans. You can buy either manually or electrically operated switches. The electric type is generally used on the main lines, and the manual type on little-used sidings or where the operator can get to them handily.

By adding a pair of switches (one left-hand and one right-hand) to a basic oval, fig. 2-18, you have a more interesting track plan because you can choose a longer or shorter route for the trains.

Another, perhaps even more interesting, arrangement using a pair of switches is shown in fig. 2-19.

So far the switches have provided some routing variety, but in only one direction of travel. By arranging the switches as shown in fig. 2-20, you create a reversing or turning track. The train will reverse itself going one way, then it must be backed through the switches to return it to its original route of travel. You could avoid this by getting another set of switches and placing a 45- or 90-degree crossing through the middle to reverse the engine—sort of a figure eight within the oval. See how things progress!

More variations. The varieties are virtually endless. Using some additional imagination, you can come up with plans that include industrial sidings, which will allow you to perform switching moves to service a variety of industries. These sidings might include some of Lionel's operating accessories. You can purchase either used accessories from the '50s or new ones like the pipe loader or diesel cleaning

Fig. 2-22. Here's a plan with a passing siding plus a reversing loop, which can keep an operator occupied for hours.

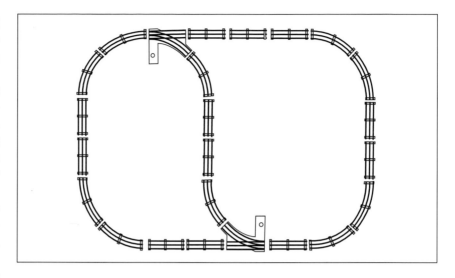

Fig. 2-20. Still another track plan variation using two switches (both right-hand in this case) provides reversing action.

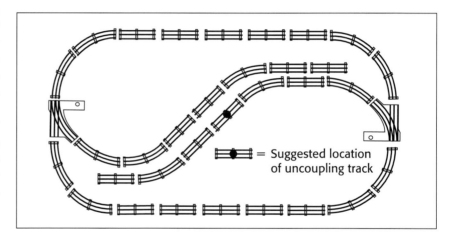

= Suggested location of uncoupling track

Fig. 2-21. A few added sidings can be used to store cars for future switching moves. An industry here and there adds action, as do accessories.

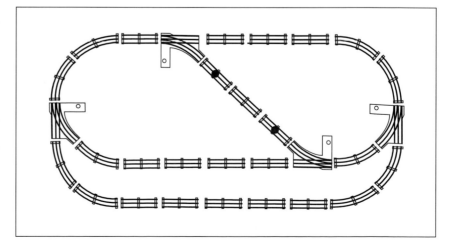

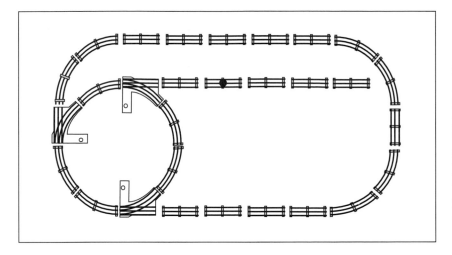

Fig. 2-23. As you can well imagine, the variations in layout design are endless. This circular loop inside the oval and a passing siding all add up to more operating fun on this layout.

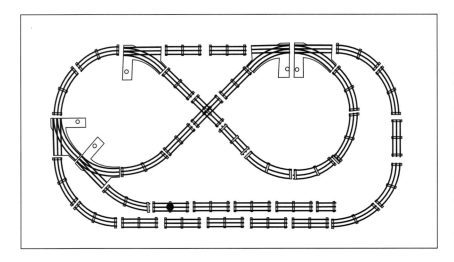

Fig. 2-24. Now you're really starting to get into it! A figure eight with an oval and a siding for storage can provide some interesting switching moves.

facility. (See Chapter Eight for more on accessories.)

These accessories are best located on sidings like those included in the plan shown in fig. 2-21. By placing an uncoupling track in these sidings, you can spot cars for loading or unloading at each industry. Between the tracks you could place a station or sheds for passengers to embark on their journey.

With the addition of even more switches, you can set up the pattern shown in fig. 2-22.

This plan has a reversing loop to add excitement to your model railroad operations. The larger passing siding can house an additional train, and the loop can reverse trains for operating variety.

Combine a large oval with an inner circle, fig. 2-23, and a siding for more running space in the same area. This loop within a loop plan includes a siding for industry and affords some switching flexibility not available on the other plans.

Finally, as shown in fig. 2-24, a figure eight inside the oval, combined with a siding for passengers or an accessory, provides the ultimate in operational variety for a small layout. Besides all this, you can hold a train or two on any of the loops, making it possible to run freight and passenger trains alternately.

These are just a few of many different track arrangements that are possible. I hope they serve to stimulate your creativity. Now it's time to try designing some plans of your own.

DESIGNING YOUR OWN LAYOUT

What do you need to design you own layout? Really nothing more than a pencil, graph paper, a track-planning template (several brands are available at hobby shops), and a strong desire to design an empire, small or large, that suits you. Get some graph paper ruled in quarter-inch squares, get out a pencil and the template (fig. 2-25), and start doodling. Use four squares to represent one foot.

You can get a lot of track even on a 4' x 8' sheet of plywood, but don't try cramming in too much. Less track creates an illusion that it's a bigger railroad. Also, keeping the track plan simple will cause you less frustration as a beginner. I want you to have fun, not frustration.

Clearances. As you're designing your plan, refer often to fig. 2-26, which shows the minimum clearance you need to allow between parallel tracks, between tracks and station platforms and lineside buildings, and for tunnels. If clearances are not adequate on all sides, your trains will bump into one another or into lineside buildings. Keep these specifications handy.

THE PROJECT TRACK PLAN

For this project layout, I decided to use the basic oval and combine it with one siding for an additional train or cars and another siding to use as an industrial spur or perhaps to serve a station or a station platform. The layout uses two pairs of switches, two uncoupling tracks that will allow you to spot cars and add switching moves, and six half-sections to eliminate cutting. See fig. 2-25.

It includes some simple scenery and, of course, a mountain in the corner that is removable so you can take the layout down after the holidays. Some buildings, an accessory or two, a road, and you're in business. I'll also show in detail the different stages of building the layout—ranging from just laying the track on the board to placing it on roadbed and then adding a bit of ballast here and there for realism. We will tackle the basic wiring, including the switches, and have trains running before you know it.

Fig. 2-25. Track-planning templates like this one made by CTT, Inc., of Dallas, Texas, make it easy to put your track planning ideas on paper. All you need is graph paper, a pencil, and the template. This plan shown is the one the author will tell you how to build, starting in the next chapter.

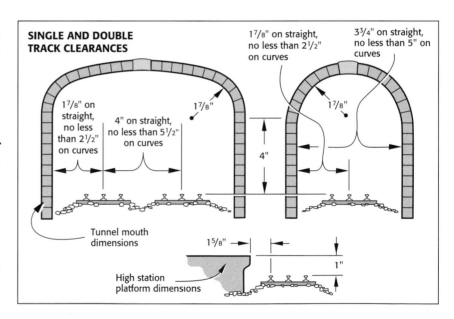

Fig. 2-26. Here are important minimum clearances to keep in mind if you're going to design your own model railroad complete with tunnels, buildings, and scenery.

CHAPTER THREE

Building a 4 x 8 Train Table

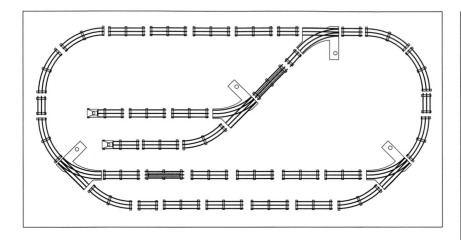

Fig. 3-1. This is the plan for the layout the author built.

LIST OF SUPPLIES

BASIC MATERIALS

9   pieces of 1x4 pine 8 feet long (layout frame)
2   pieces of 2x4 spruce 8 feet long (table legs)
1   piece 44¼" x 48" ¼ plywood (layout shelf)
1   piece 4' x 8' ⅝" exterior plywood (layout top)
1   box 1¼" drywall screws
16   3" x ¼" bolts
16   ¼ x 20 nuts
32   washers to fit

TRACK AND SWITCHES

9   65501 curved track sections
18   65500 straight track sections
6   65505 ½ straight track sections
2   65530 remote uncoupler
2   65132 remote switches (right-hand)
2   65133 remote switches (left-hand)
2   62283 die-cast illuminated bumpers
1   Lionel RS-1 transformer
2   Atlas #205 connectors

LIONEL BUILDINGS AND ACCESSORIES

1   2709 Rico station
1   12773 freight shed
1   12731 station platform
1   62180 road signs
1   12760 highway blinker
1   12831 rotating beacon
1   12714 crossing gate

SCENERY AND RELATED MATERIAL

3   boxes of Woodland Scenics trees (6" to 7")
1   Woodland Scenics yellow coarse turf
1   Woodland Scenics green coarse turf
1   Woodland Scenics scenic cement
3   bags of light gray ballast
1   bag of dark ballast
2   "Mountains in Minutes" tunnel portals
2   sheets of 2' x 8' insulating foam (mountain)
8   sections of Midwest O gauge roadbed (roads)
1   box of Life-Like grass
1   1137 Life-Like traffic accessories
1   1138 Life-Like railroad signals
1   1141 Life-Like standing people
1   1142 Life-Like station accessories
1   quart of earth tone latex paint
1   large bottle of Elmer's carpenters glue

As you learned in Chapter Two, there are many interesting track arrangement possibilities for a 4' x 8' space. The plan I've chosen to build is shown in fig. 3-1.

Before you begin construction, give some thought to where you'll set up the fully landscaped layout. If you decide to build a semi-permanent pike—one that can be moved later, or stored—space is no problem. You can unscrew the legs; remove the trains, buildings, and accessories; and store the board in the garage, in the cellar, or under a bed.

If you decide to build a permanent layout, you must allocate some space for year-round operation. When it comes to finding space for a layout, the ingenuity of some people is amazing. Over the years I've seen many Lionel trains set up in garages. One fellow right in my hometown attaches his layout to an overhead system so that when he's finished running trains, he can literally lift his layout up and out of the way. The attic is another possibility. Still another spot might be a spare room.

Since many homes in this country have a basement, that is a good place for your construction project. That's the spot that was allocated to me for this project. I'm pretty handy with tools, and know how to work with wood and plasterboard, so I first built a room for the layout. A drop ceiling, floor tile or carpeting, electrical outlets, and plenty of light fixtures are all nice additions to your train room. You'll be spending a lot of time in this room, so make it both functional and attractive.

TOOLS REQUIRED

Before you make that celebrated trip to the lumberyard, make a quick list of tools that you'll need. Keep everything

Fig. 3-2. The author's completed 4' x 8' Lionel layout with buildings and accessories identified below. See a complete list of supplies at the left.

1. 12731 station platform
2. 62180 road signs
3. 2709 Rico station
4. 12773 freight shed
5. 12760 highway blinker
6. 12831 rotary beacon
7. 12714 crossing gate

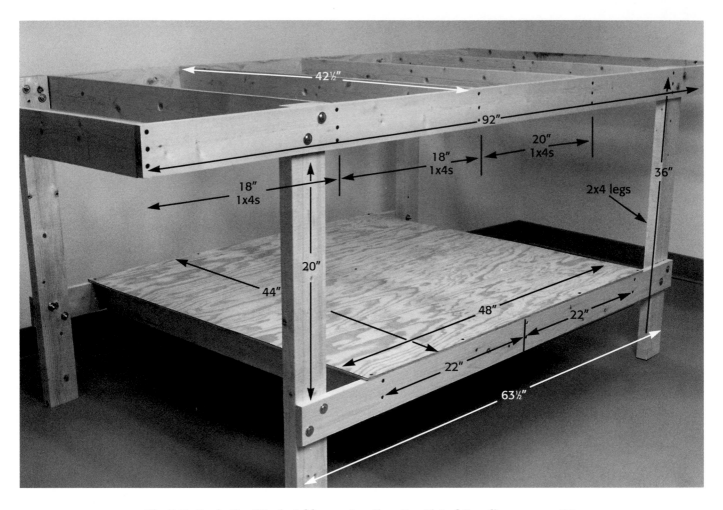

Fig. 3-3. Basic 4' x 8' train table construction. See List of Supplies on page 28.

simple is my motto, especially when it comes to building a Lionel layout. You will need a good finish handsaw. (Don't buy a crosscut saw, as they work against the grain for fast cutting and splinter the pine you'll be using.) An electric drill should also be on your list. I prefer battery-powered drills, simply because you don't have to worry about a cord getting tangled.

For this layout you will use common drywall screws to hold the train table together. This is where the drill comes in real handy. Newer drill tips contain magnets to hold the screws as you drive them home, allowing for a more precise fit on the corners. Using

drywall screws is fast, and they hold tight. (If you want to make your layout that much more secure, use a drop of yellow glue on the joints.) If you prefer nails to drywall screws, you can use them, too, but purchase serrated nails for better holding power.

Along with the drill, you'll need a no. 8 pilot drill bit to drill clearance holes for the drywall screws. Later you'll also need other small bits for drilling holes in the layout to secure the track, for electrical work, and to mount switches or possibly a transformer. You'll need a level, some pencils for marking the wood, a tape measure or folding zig-zag ruler, and a square.

Three or four C-clamps are needed to hold the legs as you level and secure the layout. I suggest you buy the ones that open to at least 6 to 8 inches.

PERMANENT OR SEMI-PERMANENT?

If you want to build a semi-permanent layout, all you have to remember is to make adjustments in the design so you can take the layout down readily after the season or after extended playing periods. If you choose a semi-perma-nent design, you'll have to fasten the legs with bolts and nuts to allow you to disassemble them easily. Track must be secured with screws, ballast glued down, and scenery securely attached so it doesn't fall to the floor when you tip the layout up for storage. Legs can be cut from 2x4s, or you can make sawhorses, like the ones you always seem to see on sale at the lumberyard. Wiring should be marked or routed in such a way that you have to unplug only two wires from the transformer for storage.

Permanent layouts, on the other hand, can be constructed differently. The ballast can be sprinkled on and left loose, instead of being glued down. Buildings and accessories can be placed permanently. Nails can be used to hold the entire train table together. Wiring can be permanently routed to the power supply via terminal strips for a neater appearance. These are the major considerations. Decide whether your layout will be permanent or semi-permanent, and you're ready to begin construction.

TRIP TO THE LUMBERYARD

Besides shopping for trains to run on your layout, one of the more exciting things to do is go to the lumberyard. Before you go however, let me give you a few tips in lumber selection and a shopping list. You will need a variety of lumber from the yard, including some finished 1x4s, 2x4s, plywood, and an assortment of nuts, bolts, washers, and screws. It's all specified in fig. 3-2.

With regard to the lumber selection, I recommend spending a little more and buying the best grade available. By staying away from the lower grades, you'll avoid problems later from wood warping or shrinking. The so-called econ-omy line in the lumber pile is more often than not "kiln dried," which acts like a sponge when it comes to moisture. We are only building a 4' x 8' layout here, and the bill for the entire project is not going to break the average working person; so my advice is to buy the best your budget will allow. You will never be sorry that you elected to stay with high-quality lumber.

Try to find a lumberyard that will cut material for you. My yard charges a mere 25 cents per cut. It's well worth the money. You'll have nice straight cuts, and the sawdust mess will be left at the lumberyard. Have all your measurements ready for the yardman; people hate to be tied up while you make a decision. Take this book with you and refer to fig. 3-2 for a bill of materials.

Some other good tips: Buy framing and plywood that has been stored inside, if possible. If you can, go to the yard mid-morning on a weekday, when business is slow. When buying "stick lumber," i.e., 1x4s or 2x4s, check the wood both ways for warping. Lay one end on the floor while holding the other end and turn it in all directions while sighting along its length. If your eyes are bad, lay the wood on the floor and turn it. Check the ends for splitting. Check the width, because it's common for finished pine to vary more than an eighth of an inch. Take a tape measure with you and measure each piece. For the tabletop, select exterior grade plywood, finished one side (sometimes referred to as being plugged and sanded), in a thickness of either ½" or ⅝". I like the lat-ter; it just makes for a stronger layout. For the storage shelf underneath, ¼" plywood is fine. For legs, my preference is 2x4s rather than 2x3s, especially on a 4' x 8' layout.

CONSTRUCTION BEGINS

After bringing your cache home, the first thing you have to determine before cutting your first piece of lumber is table height. The accepted height for most tabletop layouts comes in around 36", plus or minus a few inches due to individual tastes. Kids like this height because the trains are at their eye level and look more realistic as they go chugging by. On the other hand, 40" is good for adults because it permits easy access for reaching derailed trains or attending to scenic details as you construct your pike.

Start with the 2x4s and cut four 36" lengths for the legs. The actual table height will be 36⅝" when you attach the plywood top. See fig. 3-3. Cut the four leg pieces as precisely as you can or have the lumberyard do it for you. For a professional look, sand all splinters from the edges. Set the four legs aside for the moment.

For the outside support beams and crossbraces, round up three of those 1x4s purchased for the outside perimeter of the layout. Rather than trying to be too exact, I make the frame a little undersize. It's designed so when the top has been secured, there will be a 2" overhang all around. This overhang acts as a handle that you can grab to move the table about. It also just looks better, especially if are planning to hang fabric around the pike to

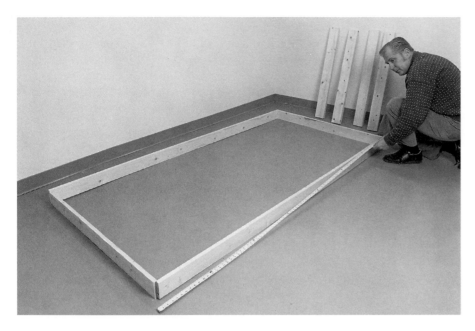

Fig. 3-4. One of the first steps in building your layout is cutting pieces to fit the 4' x 8' piece of plywood. The text gives all the dimensions.

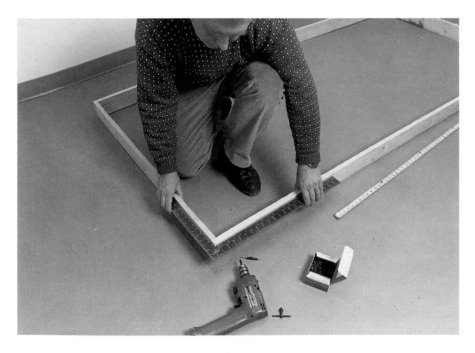

Fig. 3-5. To give your project a professional look, keep all corners square. Use a carpenter's square to make sure the frame is square.

less 4" equals 92". Now take another 1x4 and mark it at 42½". This allows for the 2"and the thickness of the wood (¾"). Lay the shorter piece down between the two longer pieces. You should wind up with an overall width of 44". See fig. 3-4. If you're off, now is the time to make corrections. If you're right on, cut another piece at 42½" and sand all edges before moving on.

The next step is to tie all four corners together as a unit. I suggest you use 1¼" no. 8 drywall screws. Before you drive them in place, drill a pilot hole so the wood doesn't split at the very end. Use a no. 8 screw pilot, which not only makes a hole for the screw but countersinks the wood to accommodate the head of the screw as well.

Take a large carpenter's square and hold it at each corner to check the squareness of the base as shown in fig. 3-5. If your concrete floor is a bit uneven, as mine is, line up the tops of the 1x4s at each corner and then install one screw at each corner. See fig. 3-6. You can, if you wish, place the large square under each corner, which will in effect level each corner for you.

After you are satisfied that all four corners are square, place another two screws in each corner to tighten things up. Keep in mind that while pine is easy to work with, it is soft; so don't drive those screws in too tight. Just flush with the outer surface is fine.

The next step is to add the interior cross members. First cut four pieces of 1x4, 42½" long. Lightly sand each end. If by chance you picked a piece of

dress it up later on. You can, if you wish, make everything flush. Use the same technique and just add a few more inches to my dimensions.

With that in mind, cut two pieces of 1x4 to 7' 8" long. We are moving the support system 2" in from either side, and the purchased length of 96" (8')

Fig. 3-6. The corners are very important. Make sure that the top part of the pine is perfectly level, so when you install the plywood top everything is smooth and level.

wood that has a very slight bend in it, this is the perfect place for it. Once the plywood is down, no one will know the difference. I placed the cross member center lines 18" and 36" from each end. This leaves me about 20" in the exact center—close enough without splitting hairs. Attach these supports in the same way as the end braces, taking care at all points of alignment. Check for levelness and install three screws at each end. Square each as you go. See fig. 3-7.

Now that the top of the framework is complete and square, flip the framework over for installation of the legs. The

legs will go on the outside of the very first support, making them roughly 16" from each end. If you use 2x3s or 2x4s for the entire frame, you have a more rigid frame, and you can place each leg at the very end.

With lighter 1x4s, legs placed toward the center support the layout more evenly.

Place the 36" 2x4 leg on the outside of the first brace—but inside the frame—and secure it temporarily with a C-clamp, as

Fig. 3-7. Left: For interior bracing, the installation of 1x4 pine will keep the plywood from sagging. Remarkably, the frame, when tied in with the ⁵⁄₈" plywood, makes a table you can sit on. Right: If someone in the family helps you lift the frame on its side, you can use a portable drill to drive the final drywall screws home.

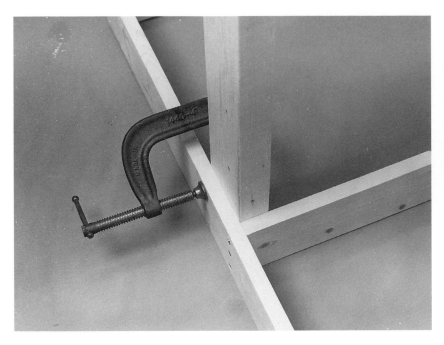

Fig. 3-8: The author used 2x4s for the legs. Here he installs them to the inside of the crossbraces, adding to the integrity of the frame. C-clamps held the legs in place until bolts were installed.

Fig. 3-9. Using a ⁵⁄₁₆″ speed bore, drill two holes for ¼″ bolts, which will secure the legs.

Fig. 3-10. Always use a washer on both ends of the bolt. It helps to keep the wood from splintering as you secure each leg.

This high-speed bit is designed to make clean holes in wood for bolts. (I used bolts to attach the legs so it would be easy to remove the legs to store the layout.) Drill two holes through the frame (fig. 3-9) and leg, roughly 45 degrees to each other. Place a washer on each bolt and insert from the frame side, as shown in fig. 3-10. Add a washer to the other end, and then thread on a nut. Hand-tighten all eight nuts; then have someone help you flip the whole assembly upright. Having an assistant lessens the chance of your breaking the frame when you transfer the weight to only two side legs during this process. Again check for squareness. If you are off a tad, don't panic. Using ¼″ bolts in the ⁵⁄₁₆″ holes you drilled with the speed bore leaves some room to adjust the legs right or left for a true vertical line. Now with a level, check all four corners, as

shown in fig. 3-8. Now raise the frame and check for squareness and topside alignment. You don't want this 2x4 sticking above the frame and hindering installation of the plywood top. Run your finger across the top of the frame and the legs to make sure both are aligned. Check the upright position with your square.

After you have the leg positioned properly, grab your drill and install a ⁵⁄₁₆″ speed bore.

Fig. 3-11. With frame laid out and secure, have someone help you tip the entire assembly up. Now you can go about the job of making sure everything is level. Slight adjustments can and should be made now. They will be difficult to make after the plywood top is on.

shown in fig. 3-11. If you are off a little, possibly because of the floor, move the layout to another part of the room and try again or bottom shim the legs to make up the difference.

The next step is to add the bottom bracing between the legs. This accomplishes a number of things. First, it steadies up the benchwork. Second, it provides a base for light shelving that can be used to store extra cars, engines, or empty boxes. Using your tape, measure the distance between the legs at the top. On my table the legs are 63½" from outside to outside Cut two pieces of 1x4 to this length.

Now measure approximately 20" down from the underside of the top 1x4. This is the height I found most convenient for the storage shelf. There is still room to get underneath to wire your layout. Hold the leg braces to the legs with C-clamps, as shown in fig. 3-12. Next, drill holes for the bolts and install washers, bolts, and nuts, as you did to attach the legs to the frame. Use two bolts per leg.

For the shelf, use a 4' x 4' sheet of ¼" plywood. At most yards these are simply called "handy panels." Have the yard rip one side to a width of 44". Now cut three pieces of 1x4 exactly 42½" long for the inside bracing of this shelf.

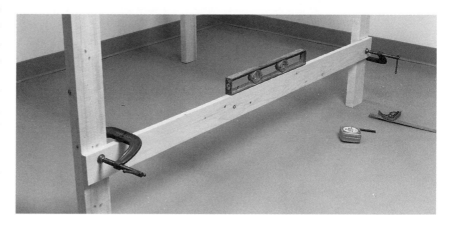

Fig. 3-12. Adding the storage shelf is next. After cutting 1x4s to the dimensions specified in the text, C-clamp the first support prior to drilling and bolting.

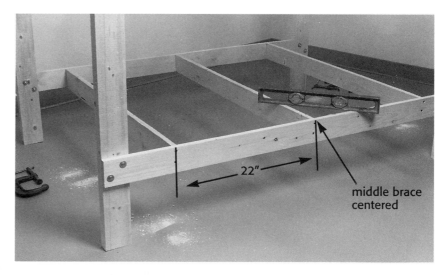

Fig. 3-13. With the storage shelf frame bolted on, a level check is in order. Note that by using bolts, the entire shelf can be removed for storage.

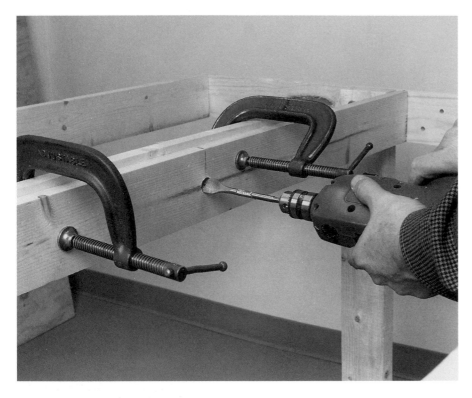

Fig. 3-14. A handy way to route wires under the platform is to simply drill a single hole right down the middle. Using C-clamps, attach a spare piece of pine to the backside to keep the speed bore from splitting the drilled piece of wood.

Fig. 3-15. Without the top, this is how the project should look up to now. If you want to stain the wood, this would be a good time to do it.

Now find the center of the span between the legs and place your first cross member there. Measure 22" from this mark toward each leg and make another mark. Install the three cross members as shown in fig. 3-13. If you like to be really exact, you can measure out far enough so that the plywood runs flush, but if your carpentry is off a bit, it will show. Besides, the 22" measurement will again give you a 2" lip to hold on to when you want to disassemble the shelf.

Before you place the bottom shelf on the table, find the middle of the top inner four cross members and drill a ¾" hole in each. This will be the wire run as you hook up track, switches, and accessories. It will be neater than having wires hanging in the way later.

When drilling those holes with a speed bore, it is always a good idea to back the drilled piece of wood with another piece of scrap wood, as shown in fig. 3-14. It will prevent the drilled piece from splitting as the drill penetrates the outer side. This will be important later on, when you're wiring the layout; there is nothing worse than feeding wires through those holes and getting a handful of splinters in the process.

The completed table is shown in fig. 3-15 prior to adding the plywood top. Finish the shelf by placing the plywood down and securing with some drywall screws. I've found that a few no. 8 drywall screws along each edge plus a few down the center is enough.

If everything is now square, you can move on to the final

Fig. 3-16. Install drywall screws around the perimeter of the top. Also, mark your center braces and run some screws down the middle to keep the plywood from bowing later.

phase of table construction—adding the plywood top. Place the plywood on top of the frame and check to see that you have at least 2" all around. When the top is properly positioned, fasten it to the frame with drywall screws placed every 12" or so, as shown in fig. 3-16. A carpenter's square set at 2⅜", fig. 3-17, will keep you in the center of the 1x4. Find the center of your crossbraces and screw the top to them also.

Since plywood is a laminate, there may be a tendency for the sheet to buckle or bow in certain areas. A few additional screws in the right places will take care of that.

With the benchwork complete, we're ready to move on to the basics of track and switches. Then we can start to run trains!

Fig. 3-17. Using an adjustable square, set the distance from the edge of the plywood to the center of the 1x4 pine frame and mark the line where you'll install the drywall screws. If you did everything right, it should come to 2⅜" from the edge to the center of the pine frame supports.

CHAPTER FOUR

Laying Track

Fig. 4-1. Here we go! With the table secure, set up the basic track plan, install a lockon, connect wires to a transformer, and run some trains.

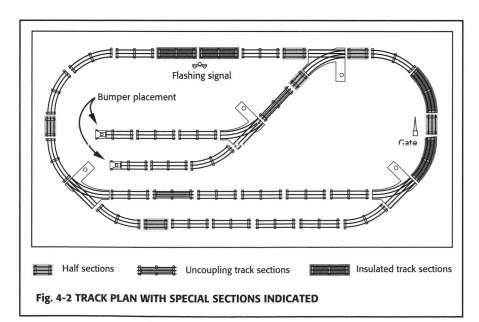

Flashing signal

Bumper placement

Gate

Half sections   Uncoupling track sections   Insulated track sections

Fig. 4-2 TRACK PLAN WITH SPECIAL SECTIONS INDICATED

With the benchwork out of the way, you're ready to lay some track and get to the fun of running trains.

There are three or four methods of laying track. As a beginner, you're naturally interested in the simplest. But since they are all easy, I'll review them quickly.

The first—and easiest—method is merely to lay the track on the plywood base and screw it down after you have the track arranged the way you want it.

The second method is to fasten a 4' x 8' sheet of ¾" Homasote (a board made from recycled newspaper) to the plywood. This will become a sound-absorbing base on which to mount your track.

A third approach is to add cork roadbed between the track and the plywood. The cork helps to quiet the noise of the trains and raises the track up on a roadbed, making your layout more realistic. Cork roadbed for O gauge track is sold in hobby shops.

I'll explain how to lay the track for a specific plan, but these methods will work for other plans as well. This track plan consists of an oval with two spurs and an attached siding that allows trains to pass one another.

Later, as your collection of rolling stock grows, you might consider cutting off the power within the siding or spur tracks for engine storage. That will be discussed a bit later in the electrical section of this book.

INITIAL TRACK ASSEMBLY

Gather the O gauge track items needed for your layout, and you're ready to begin. See the List of Supplies in Chapter Three. Start by joining the track sections to make sure they fit. See figs. 4-1 and 4-2.

It doesn't matter where you start the track-laying process. With this plan, I suggest that you start at the front section. Then you can position the switches at the ends of the curves as you work around the 4' x 8' sheet of plywood.

As you progress, you will finish the outer loop, placing the curved track, straight track, and half sections as indicated in fig. 4-2. No track cutting is required for this plan.

In order to do some switching of cars, I suggest installing two uncoupling track sections at the locations specified in fig. 4-2. The one in the lead to the industrial sidings enables you to spot cars on either track.

The other uncoupling track is located in the passing siding. You will eventually be able to operate two trains on the layout (although not at the same time). A train longer than the passing siding may be operated, but doing so will cause a storage problem on the inner siding. The uncoupling track in the passing siding will enable you to break the train and park the engine and a few extra cars on the industrial siding or team track.

After the track is assembled, install illuminated bumpers on the ends of the industrial sidings, as shown in fig. 4-3.

Fig. 4-3. Install illuminated bumpers at the ends of the sidings.

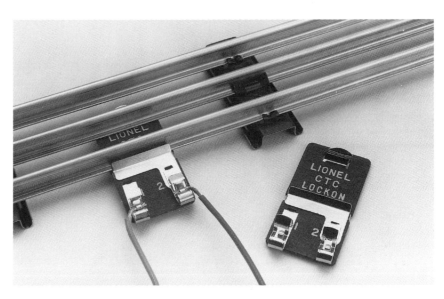

Fig. 4-4. To supply power to the track, Lionel makes a lockon that clips on to the track. Two wires from the transformer supply power.

HOOK UP A TRANSFORMER

By this time you're ready to run trains. Go to it! To power your train, you'll need a train transformer. If you received one with your train set, go ahead and use it. Later on you may want to upgrade and invest in a transformer that's a little more versatile. These are readily available at any model railroad shop. I highly recommend the top-of-the-line Lionel RS-1, which has two solid-state throttles for trains and accessories and control buttons for the bell, horn or whistle, and direction.

Place a temporary lockon on the track (fig. 4-4), hook one wire to number 1, one to number 2, and attach these to the red (#1) and black (#2) terminals of the Lionel RS-1 or to the appropriate connecting posts on the transformer that came with the set.

Fig. 4-5. This is the right-hand side of the layout with the track in place. The rotary beacon is in place. The Rico station, still in the box, is in its intended position, as is the crossing gate. The transformer is in a temporary location; later it will be moved to a proper control panel.

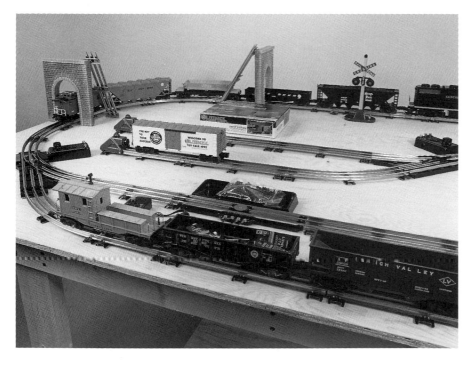

Fig. 4-6. Things are starting to shape up. This is how the left-hand side of the layout looks with the basics down. Cars are being tested for clearance, switches are set, and uncoupling sections are in place. The freight station is still in its box, but in position.

TAKE A TEST DRIVE

Place a locomotive on the track, along with a few cars and a caboose, and open the throttle. The switches and uncoupling tracks will not operate without their respective controllers, of course. If you want to experiment with the uncoupling tracks, hook up the wires according to the instructions and operate them, using controllers placed temporarily on top of the benchwork. Later you'll install the controllers more permanently.

TEMPORARILY PLACE BUILDINGS

After you've had some fun, take a break and consider a few additional items. You may want to consider doing things a little differently than I did. If you decide to use different buildings or accessories, think about their placement now, as you start to visualize the location of other buildings, roads, and grade crossings. As you can see in fig. 4-5, I've placed a Lionel Rico station by the transformer, along with a station platform for the passengers. A rotating beacon will have a spot to the right rear of the railroad. A freight station will occupy one of the team tracks, fig. 4-6.

CHECKING CLEARANCES

Later, you will build a mountain in one corner of the layout with a tunnel through it; now is a good time to check for clearances. Temporarily prop the tunnel portals in place and run your longest freight cars or engines back and forth, making sure they don't sideswipe the inside of the tunnel. Reposition the

Fig. 4-7. As you start to lay track, you should plan ahead to mountain construction. You can position temporary tunnel portals to check clearances of engines and cars. After you are set, it's a good idea to mark the bases of the portals on the plywood for reference.

Fig. 4-8. Don't forget to look on both sides of the portal, making sure your largest or longest piece of rolling stock will fit through.

portals if they do. See figs. 4-7 and 4-8. I used tunnel portals made by Mountains in Minutes. They are made for scale railroads, and therefore the interior dimensions tend to be a bit tighter; but they are readily available at most hobby shops and work just fine if placed right. Lionel portals are wider but difficult to find because Lionel has not made them in years. Other brands of tunnel portals for "hi-rail" layouts are

available. A little scouting in your area will turn them up.

Buildings, station platforms, and lineside warning signals pose less of a clearance problem because these items can be moved back from the tracks if necessary. The only potential problem area is between the twin tracks and the passing siding, but the station platforms fit here with the greatest of ease, as shown in fig. 4-9.

This might be a good time to

temporarily place a few figures and details around the layout, fig. 4-10. Now you can imagine what the layout will look like when it's finished.

INSULATED TRACK SECTIONS

Before fastening the track for good, you might want to buy or make a few insulated track sections. They will be used to operate trackside accessories like the flasher and

Fig. 4-9. Check station platform clearances by placing them in the proper position and then running trains by them to see that they clear.

Fig. 4-10. With the track down, it's time to run trains (for testing of course) and have some fun. A few people here and there will add interest even at this state.

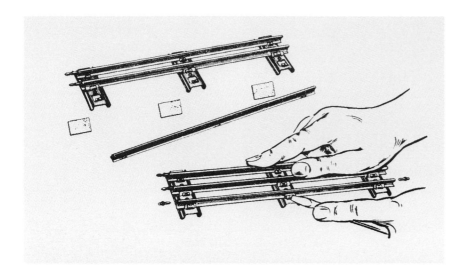

Fig. 4-11. Lionel now has factory-made insulated track sections on the market. But making your own insulated track is quick, easy, and very inexpensive. Refer to this drawing and the text.

crossing gate. The locations of these insulated track sections are specified in fig. 4-2.

You can purchase insulated track sections or make your own. All you need is a flat-blade screwdriver and a few bits of insulation from old or discarded track. To start, lay the section of track—either straight or curved—on a flat surface and carefully pry up the tabs on the outside rail. (You don't want to slip and hurt yourself.) See fig. 4-11. Next, take the rail out of the tie slots and place short pieces of insulation on the rail so that it doesn't make contact with the black metal tie again. You can use Lionel insulation, a matchbook cover, or a double thickness of a file card.

Before placing this insulated track section back on line, pull the standard metal track pins, fig. 4-12, on each end of the insulated rail and replace them with two insulated pins. See fig. 4-13. The insulated pins will block the electrical current to this side of the track section, in effect making the adjoining rails a self-contained "electrical switch." The metal wheels of the Lionel cars will complete the circuit. See fig. 4-14.

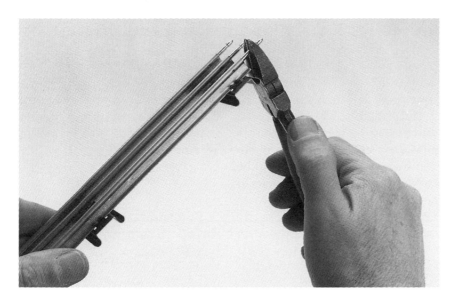

Fig. 4-12. To remove or replace track pins, pull them out neatly with a wire cutter at this angle. Rock the pliers so it acts as a lever against the tie.

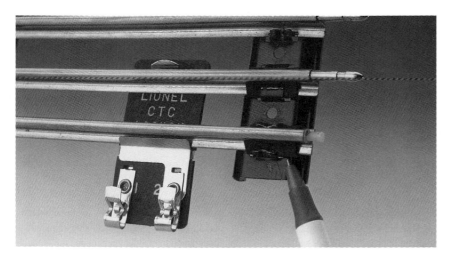

Fig. 4-13. Closeup photograph shows the position of the lockon (for power to that section), the insulation, and the insulating pin.

Fig. 4-14. The grade crossing flasher is positioned on the layout, and an insulated track section has been installed. Later we'll wire the circuit so an approaching train activates the grade crossing flasher.

CREATING BLOCKS

Finally, you should consider creating electrically isolated blocks now, before fastening the track. By "blocking" the layout, as shown in fig. 4-15, you'll be able to park one train while running another. To be able to run two trains, you need to have a way to insulate sections of track, or blocks, so that you can turn the power to that section off or on, energizing one train or another.

You'll use the sidings as holding tracks. So after you are through running and testing trains, you have to install insulated pins in each middle rail at each end of the passing siding and at the top of the industrial spur. See figs. 14-16 and 4-17. Later you can mount

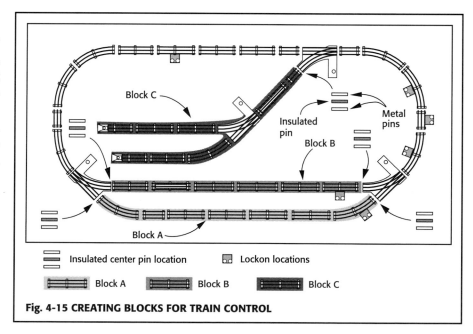

Fig. 4-15 CREATING BLOCKS FOR TRAIN CONTROL

a toggle or sliding switch in the control panel to switch them on or off. For now, though, you can "jump" each lockon by

Fig. 4-16. As blocks are established, place insulated track pins in the center rails to block the transfer of electricity from one section of the track to another.

Fig. 4-17. To test a block, place a lockon in the section. To energize the track, connect a wire to clip #1. The outside rails are left as is with metal pins.

placing a wire from the transformer (red side) to number 1 on the lockon, which will energize that middle track.

FASTENING TRACK

After creating the insulated track sections and blocks, you're ready to fasten the track in place permanently. You have some options here. You can screw the track down after you've measured all around the table for straightness and uniformity. Later, in the chapter on scenery, you'll learn how to ballast the track for a touch of realism and bond it in place.

Another method is to place roadbed between the track and plywood (fig. 4-18) to act as a moderate sound absorber and to raise the track slightly, allowing you to pile ballast in true prototype fashion. You will purchase O gauge cork roadbed in 3' lengths and split it down the middle for ease of installation, especially around curves. If you're going to use roadbed, you'll need to mark the position of all your track, remove it, glue the roadbed down with Elmer's yellow glue, wait a few hours, and then replace the track. Cork roadbed is cheaper by the box. (Each box covers 75 running feet.)

Fasten the track to the plywood top (with or without the roadbed option) with no. 4 x ¾" roundhead or pan screws in every other track section, as shown in fig. 4-19. When that's done, you're ready for the next step in the project—electrical wiring.

Fig. 4-18. If you decide to use roadbed, you can buy cork roadbed in 3-foot lengths, pull it apart to make it easier to negotiate curves, and glue it all down. You'll attach and secure the track later.

Fig. 4-19. The track should be screwed down for security. Every other section is fine; alternate sides of the tie. Use no. 4 x ¾" screws with either round or pan heads. Do not tighten the screws down too tightly, since this can bend the ties and cause the rail to become out of gauge.

CHAPTER FIVE

Power Up!

Electricity is to model railroaders what coal and diesel fuel are to the real thing. It powers our trains. Currently—no pun intended—Lionel trains run on low voltage AC (alternating current) in the range of 8 to 18 volts, depending upon the engine or accessories used. This voltage is produced by a transformer, which lowers the average 115-volt house current to manageable and safe levels and delivers it to the track via a speed control. The control operates in much the same way as the accelerator pedal in your car—push it down and the car goes faster, let it up and the car slows down. The same happens when using a transformer. As you turn the lever or knob up, the train speeds up; as you turn the lever down, the train slows for a station or a complete stop. It's as simple as that. Or is it?

Since this is a beginner's book, I won't get too complicated in my explanation of wiring. I'll just cover the basics and explain some electrical terms. The emphasis will be on wiring and operating the 4' x 8' layout we're building. I'll explain simple block controls, discuss how to install operating accessories, and tell you why switch machines and uncoupling tracks work much better on constant voltage. We will also get into accessory lighting, so your railroad will look realistic for nighttime running. I'll show you how to

Fig. 5-1. The control panel built by the author provides the operator with fingertip access to the transformer and all other switches and controllers.

Fig. 5-2. Transformers come in a number of shapes, sizes, and power ratings. From the left clockwise, the contemporary RS-1 by Lionel Trains Inc., the ZW by the older Lionel Corporation, and a smaller, less powerful 4851 unit often placed in Lionel train sets.

build a control panel (fig. 5-1) so everything will be within reach when you're the "engineer" running the trains.

As you read along, you'll see that I like to provide a foundation of basic knowledge and then explain the how-to part.

AMPS, VOLTS, WATTS

To start out, electricity is measured in three ways: amperes, volts, and watts. Amperes or amps are a measure of the quantity of electrical current flowing through a circuit. A good example of the power at work here is your car battery. Although the battery is only rated at 12 volts, the amps are very high, sometimes in the neighborhood of 600 amps plus for big cars with many options.

Volts, on the other hand, are a measure of electrical pressure. If your transformer takes 115 volts from the line inside the house and lowers it to safe train levels of about 8 to 18 volts, we say that the voltage has been stepped down. The throttle control on the transformer delivers the volts to the track. This voltage is the pressure that forces the current through the circuit, making your engine or accessories operate.

Lastly, watts are a measurement of electrical power, equal to volts times amps. If you're running a train at 15 volts and it's drawing 1 amp of current, the power being used is 15 watts (15v x 1a). Some Lionel operators like to include a voltmeter and ammeter as part of their control panel.

Lionel transformers that have been made run the spectrum from 50 watts (like the RS-1 we're using) to high-output ZW transformers that deliver upwards of 275 watts of power, depending upon the load put on their power supply.

SELECTING A TRANSFORMER

Toy train operators have been blessed with plenty of good equipment over the years. When you start to really get involved in the hobby, you will probably be going to train shows or meets around your state or even around the country. As your layout grows, you'll be looking for more power to run your empire, and most likely you'll hear about Lionel's big KW and ZW transformers (fig. 5-2), which are no longer made.

Used ones can be purchased at hobby shops or train shows, but be careful. Make sure you get some kind of a bill of sale or warranty for the transformer. Most people I have dealt with over the years are fair and square. In fact, some people who deal in used transformers check them over and replace defective components to insure your safety and the proper operation of the trains on your layout. Nevertheless, be on the lookout for those misguided individuals who would rather turn a fast buck than be sure you are out of harm's way. Don't ask one question before purchasing used transformers—ask many.

All new Lionel engines and accessories are built to run as efficiently as possible, so you can be content at present with the transformer supplied with your train set or our upgrade, the Lionel RS-1.

Whether you have an older-type transformer or a newer RS-1, internally they are all basically the same. When the transformer is turned on, 115 volts is supplied to the primary winding. Inside the transformer is an iron core with two sets of wires, insulated from each other, wound around it. The primary (house current) consists of many turns of fine wire wound around this core. The secondary consists of fewer turns of heavier wire. If you counted the secondary turns, you would probably find there are approximately a fifth as many as on the primary. This device is called a "step-down" transformer, since the voltage coming out of the power supply is lowered to a safe level for operation of locomotives, lighted cars, and numerous accessories.

In fact, some older transformers can be "tapped" at various points of the winding to deliver different levels of voltage. The older Lionel 1033 transformer has four posts on top. You can get 5 to 16 volts with the A/U combination of terminals, or from 0 to 11 volts with the B/U combination. If you want to hook up for running trains, the first combination is best; for lighted accessories the second gets the nod. Don't forget, many Lionel accessories include a light bulb. Even though bulbs are rated at 18 volts, they last longer operated at lower voltages.

THE LIONEL RS-1

Before we start to wire the layout, let's discuss the power requirements and the features of the Lionel RS-1, our primary source of power.

There has been much talk in the hobby about the power re-

Fig. 5-3. The current top-of-the-line Lionel RS-1 has all the features you need to run your present railroad and to expand. If necessary, the accessory voltage knob (upper left) can be used to run a second train. With an off-on switch and controls for your horn, bell, and direction, this unit has no peer in the Lionel lineup. On the rear of the RS-1 you'll find a terminal strip for the track and accessory hookups, and a circuit breaker for protection, should you have a short circuit.

quirements of any railroad, and formulas have been devised to calculate those requirements. For the 4' x 8' layout you're building, the Lionel RS-1 has plenty of punch. At the most, you'll be operating one engine and maybe a lighted caboose at one time. So far, so good! What's more, your engines will most probably have the newer truck-mounted efficient motors. They operate at approximately half the throttle setting of older engines with "Pull-Mor" or dual motors.

The switch machines and uncoupling tracks will be hooked up to the auxiliary circuit, and both of these items will operate in very brief bursts. The added lights around our town pose no problems, nor does the flashing signal, crossing gate, or rotating beacon. At a rating of 50 watts, the RS-1 can operate everything on the layout simultaneously.

The Lionel RS-1 has plenty of features to please both beginner and veteran. To try out your RS-1, connect two wires terminating in stereo clips from the TRACK terminals (fig. 5-3) to a lockon on the layout. Place a locomotive on the track. After plugging in the RS-1, turn the transformer on by rocking the off-on switch to the "power" position. See fig. 5-3. The green light will come on, denoting that the RS-1 is operational.

After that, ease open the throttle. If the engine lights up but does not move forward or backward, hit the DIRECTION button, located on the bottom row of buttons on the left-hand side. The engine will either move forward or in reverse, depending upon which way you set the locomotive's internal control when you last operated it.

This brings up the directional control feature located in the locomotive. On most

Lionel locomotives, the direction is controlled by either a solid-state reversing unit or Lionel's older "E" unit. With either device, when power is applied, the locomotive has a cycle of responses that it goes through in order. It can be in neutral (power on, but not moving), forward, neutral, reverse, neutral, forward, and so on and on.

While this may seem like an awkward way to change direction, it does have advantages. One benefit is that if you stop the engine on the track and place it in neutral, the engine's lights will still be on (excellent for photography), and you can still blow the horn or whistle.

If you operate your locomotive with stop-and-go stations, you'll need to manually set the E-unit in the forward mode only, so when the engine automatically stops for the station and the timer has run its course, the engine will go forward without having to repeat its entire cycle.

After the train starts to move, you can control sounds built into the engine or cars with either the HORN/WHISTLE or BELL buttons. Your Lionel engine will respond to one or both, depending on how it is equipped. For instance, if you are fortunate to have an engine or special car equipped with RAILSOUNDS, you can sound the horn and energize the bell without the use of the separate no. 5904 or no. 5906 sound buttons. If you have the RS-1, don't even wire these additional controls to the track.

Next, the ACCESSORY VOLTAGE control does just what its name implies. It controls the voltage used to power the constant-voltage switch machines, uncoupling tracks, city lights, and accessories. Naturally, you will have to find a happy medium, since some accessories operate at a lower voltage than others. You can also operate a second train (in lieu of accessories) from this control, but you will have to turn the control to "off" to change direction of the locomotive. The DIRECTION button does not work on this circuit.

Additional features on the RS-1 include a circuit breaker located on the rear of the case to protect the unit from overloads caused by crossed wires (we all do that once in a while), derailed rolling stock, or a short somewhere down the line in the form of track screws, nails, or even tinsel across the tracks. It can be reset after 15 to 20 seconds. The RS-1 also has three indicator lights for POWER, ACCY (accessory), and TRACK. The latter two

get brighter as you increase the voltage to the accessories or track. Wires for either are hooked up from the rear of this transformer by means of stereo clips—red for hot or plus, black for neutral or minus.

SAFETY TIPS

Before you begin building the control panel and wiring the layout, consider the following safety tips, courtesy of Lionel Trains, Inc.:

• Read all instructions supplied with your transformer.

• This transformer (or any others) is not recommended for children younger than eight years of age.

• On a regular basis, parents should inspect the transformer for potential hazards and have the necessary repairs made by an authorized Lionel Service Center.

• This transformer is intended to be used indoors. Do not use if water is present. Serious injury can result.

• Do not use this transformer for other than its intended purpose. This unit was designed to operate with Lionel AC locomotives.

• This transformer was designed to operate on 120-volt, 60-hertz power.

• Do not operate this transformer with a damaged cord, plug, or case.

• Do not risk electrical shock by disassembling the unit. Take the unit to a Lionel Service Center.

• CAUTION! Do not leave your layout unattended, as stalled trains or obstructed accessories may overheat, resulting in damage to your layout.

• If the circuit breaker trips, return all controls to the OFF

position. Otherwise, resetting the breaker may cause the train to surge forward, throwing it off the track and hurling it to the floor.

• Unplug the transformer when not in use.

BUILDING THE CONTROL PANEL

As master of your railroad, you need a spot where you can stand (or sit) with your transformer and other controls grouped within easy reach so you can control your creation. Hence, you need to build a control panel. I believe my methods are pretty straightforward, but if you have another way of building the panel, by all means use it.

My control-panel design involves hanging the supports from under the benchwork, then leading them out to support a shelf with a moderate overhang on which to set the transformer and mount the controls. See fig. 5-1. The hanging straps will be on the inboard side of the stringers so that all wiring and terminal strips can be mounted on the outboard side, if desired, for ease of access. This will save you the trouble of working over the storage shelf as you wire your pike. The location of the panel—on either the right- or left-hand side of the layout—is such that the wiring from all but one of the Lionel controllers (used to control switch machines and uncoupling tracks) will be able to reach all the units without being spliced.

If you don't feel up to building this panel (it really is pretty simple), you can mount the transformer on the right-hand corner of the layout.

Fig. 5-4. This photograph shows how the control panel pieces go together. Using the measurements listed in the text, you can build something like this in no time at all.

Some of the block controls can be mounted right next to the transformer, and others on the left-hand corner. With this arrangement two people can operate the layout. You be the "engineer" and your partner the "dispatcher," with controls for switching and uncoupling at his or her disposal. You will, however, need to splice some of the wiring because the cables supplied with some of Lionel's track accessories will not quite reach from one end of this layout to the other.

You'll need roughly 10' of 1x4 to make the supports for the control panel. Cut four pieces 6¾" long. They will serve as hanging straps. Now cut two pieces 22½" long for the load-bearing members. Two cross members are required for the shelf. Cut them to a length

of 17⅜". The stringer spacing on your table may be slightly different than mine, so measure to confirm the length before cutting. Sand all the edges, and you're ready to assemble the control-panel platform. See fig. 5-4.

Get out your no. 8 pilot drill, no. 8 x 1¼" drywall screws, and some Elmer's yellow glue. This glue will be applied to all hanging members and to all joints for added strength. Mark both boards as shown in fig. 5-5.

Remember to make the hangers go in opposite directions, because you will be attaching them from inside rather than outside the table stringers. Use both yellow glue and screws for a secure bond. See fig. 5-6. It's a good idea to put two screws in at a time—alternating as you tighten them—as the glue tends to be slippery, which allows the hangers to move as you try to align them according to plan. Also, be careful when using an electric

Fig. 5-5. Measure and line up the upright supports. The "X" marks the spot; add glue and a few drywall screws to fasten securely.

Fig. 5-6. Put in two screws at a time, tightening them alternately. Here's how the completed supports look with upright hangers attached.

Fig. 5-7. With the major part of the panel complete, you are ready to install it under the table. The panel frame unit is made from 1x4 pine, which is readily available at any local lumberyard.

Fig. 5-8. By using this mounting arrangement, the panel will actually support itself when installed under the bench without the rocking associated with some other installation methods.

drill. You don't want to slip and run off the board and onto the floor, hurting you or someone around you.

Next, add the crossbraces that will support the whole affair. Apply glue to mating surfaces and screw them in place, as shown in fig. 5-7. Set the entire assembly aside for a few hours to allow the glue to dry.

Position the panel assembly under the layout, making sure the forward brace touches the inside part of the long (8') table

stringer, as shown in fig. 5-8. This alone adds a surprising amount of stability to the control panel, especially in reducing back-and-forth movement.

When the assembly is the way you want it, drive home two drywall screws in each upright support. Since you may want to remove the control panel when storing the layout, don't glue any part that comes in contact with the layout. The control panel frame is shown mounted to the table in fig. 5-9.

Add a panel shelf made from a piece of plywood, Masonite, or a 1" x 12" piece of pine, as I did. Attach it with screws, as shown in fig. 5-10. Stain the top side if you want to keep finger marks down to a minimum. For convenience, you may want to drill a few ½" or ¾" holes through the bottom rear of the panel for wiring later.

WIRING THE LAYOUT

To wire the layout, assemble the following items:

Fig. 5-9. Here's how the frame looks when secured to the benchwork.

Fig. 5-10. A piece of pine completes the assembly, ready for staining if you wish.

- All accessories to be used on the layout
- 7 Lionel lockons (They will be removed later if you solder all wires.)
- 1 spool of no. 18 or no. 20 gauge wire in each of the following colors: red, black, yellow, and green (from hobby shop or electronics store)
- 2 terminal strips (from Radio Shack)
- 2 Atlas Custom Line no. 205 connectors (hobby shop)
- 1 Crimping tool and assorted connectors (optional)

Miscellaneous items include a wire stripper, screwdriver, soldering iron, and solder. You also need screws for the controllers. And don't forget all your instruction sheets for track switches, uncoupling tracks, the transformer, and operating accessories.

COLOR-CODED WIRING

One of the first things to think about before wiring this or any other layout is to establish some kind of wiring code. I first came upon this idea when reading about how Lionel built its 1949 display layout in New York City, and have been using it for years. While it is not a new or hot idea, it does have merit and should be considered.

For all hot leads from the transformer to the track for train control, I use a red coated wire. For all accessory hot leads, I use yellow. For constant voltage to switch machines and uncoupling tracks, I use green. For the common or return ground, I use black. By using color-coded wires, it's easy to trace any problems. And when you add an accessory, everything just falls in line.

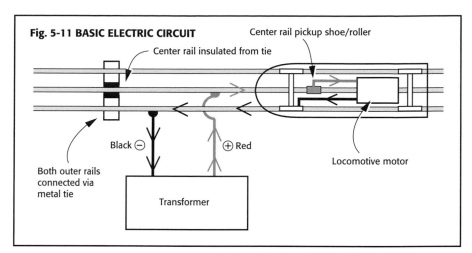

Fig. 5-11 BASIC ELECTRIC CIRCUIT

Center rail pickup shoe/roller
Center rail insulated from tie
Black ⊖   ⊕ Red
Both outer rails connected via metal tie
Transformer
Locomotive motor

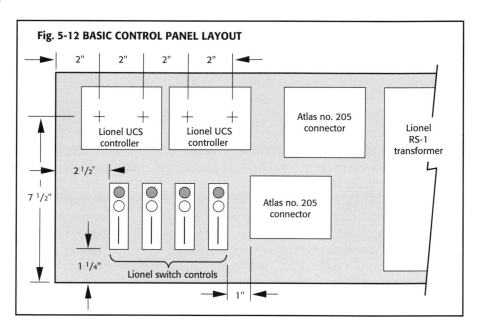

Fig. 5-12 BASIC CONTROL PANEL LAYOUT

2" 2" 2" 2"
Lionel UCS controller
Lionel UCS controller
Atlas no. 205 connector
Lionel RS-1 transformer
2 1/2"
7 1/2"
Atlas no. 205 connector
1 1/4"
Lionel switch controls
1"

BASIC ELECTRICAL CIRCUIT

As you start, keep one principle in mind. When electric current goes out (the plus [+] side) to track, accessories, or layout lighting, it must return (the minus [-] side). Always visualize that for all intents and purposes electricity travels in some sort of a circle. The current leaves the transformer, goes to work (locomotive motor, light bulbs, signals, etc.), and returns—one way or another—to the source. (See fig. 5-11.)

This one grain of wisdom, which I learned many years ago, has been the basis of my electrical savvy and has helped greatly in wiring layouts not only for myself but for friends. If for some reason you're not sure, grab a pencil and paper and sketch the circuit out. Remember: red out, black return.

CONTROL PANEL LAYOUT

As you progress with your initial wiring, remember that everything is on a temporary basis. I suggest you use Lionel lockons to get power to the track until you have all circuits working to a T. When everything is working properly, you

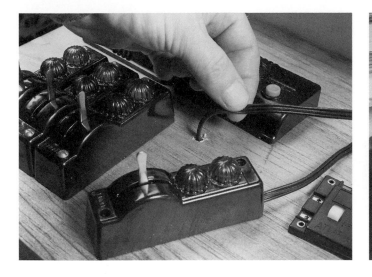

Fig. 5-13. Wires from the control panel can be routed underneath for neatness and easy tracing later on. Before installing the controller, drill a ¼" hole behind and slightly inward of where it will be mounted.

Fig. 5-14. If you follow the diagram in fig. 5-12, the control panel should look like this when completed. The author stained the top of the panel so it would be easier to clean.

may wish to remove the lock-ons and solder all connections for a more permanent attachment. (Later you'll be adding ties, and the lockons will be in the way.) The choice, or upgrade, is yours.

Begin by attaching the two terminal strips directly on the benchwork near the panel. They will aid in the placement and routing of all wires. I purchased mine at Radio Shack (part number 274-674). It is an eight-position, dual-row barrier strip that suits our needs perfectly.

Next, start to set up the control panel the way you want it. Decide where you want to place the transformer, uncoupling and switch machine controls, and Atlas off-on switches (connectors). The way I arranged the panel components is shown in fig. 5-12.

I mounted the uncoupling controls on the top left with two no. 4 x ¾" screws for each control. The units themselves will slide around the head of the screw. By merely tweaking

the clearance between the panel and the screw head, you can get a nice comfortable fit. Before fastening the units down for keeps, drill a ¼" hole behind and slightly inward of the controller for the wires to drop down and through the panel, as shown in fig. 5-13.

Next, mount the switch control boxes with no. 5 x 1½" screws through the pre-drilled holes in each. Again, mark for wires, drill the hole, and drop everything through the panel.

Important point: As you open each plastic bag that houses a controller, remove the constant-voltage plug and place it next to a switch machine for later use.

All that is left are the Atlas 205 connectors. I placed them directly to the left of the transformer to control both the track blocks and the accessories. The jog between the two 205s was intentional. I use one for train control and one for accessories, and this jog makes it easier to remember which is which. Fasten the Atlas con-

nectors to the panel with screws. Finally, place the RS-1 in its position and drill two small holes behind it for the main feeder wires. The completed control panel is shown in fig. 5-14.

BLOCK WIRING

Now you're ready to begin the actual wiring. Cut one 2' length of red wire, one 2' length of yellow wire, and two 2' lengths of black wire. Attach these wires to the back of the transformer—red and black to TRACK, yellow and black to ACCY. Run these wires down and through the control panel. Attach the yellow wire to the bottom of terminal no. 1 of the terminal strip, the accessory ground (black) to no. 8, the track ground (black) to no. 9, and the hot track lead (red) to no. 16, as shown in fig. 5-15. Note that there's plenty of room left on the terminal strips for future layout expansion.

Take a pair of red and black wires and run them from the uppermost part of the terminal

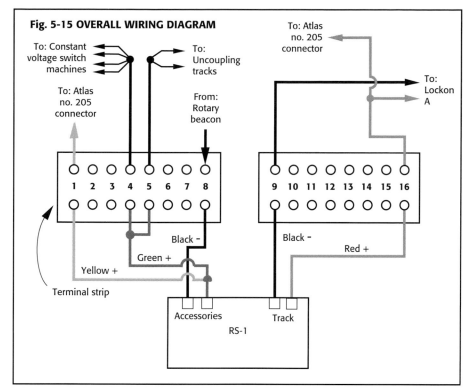

Fig. 5-15 OVERALL WIRING DIAGRAM

To: Constant voltage switch machines

To: Uncoupling tracks

To: Atlas no. 205 connector

From: Rotary beacon

To: Atlas no. 205 connector

To: Lockon A

1 2 3 4 5 6 7 8   9 10 11 12 13 14 15 16

Black –   Black –

Green +   Red +

Yellow +

Terminal strip

Accessories   Track

RS-1

Fig. 5-17. If you want to keep your layout semi-permanent, the Lionel lockons might be the way to go. However, the author recommends that you solder the wires to the track for greater reliability.

Block A

Block D

Block C

Block B

A

Red +

Black –

C

B

No. 9 on strip   No. 16 on strip

Block A
Block B
Block C
Block D

Insulated third rail

Atlas 205

RS-1

Fig. 5-16 BLOCK CONTROL WIRING

strip (no. 9 and no. 16) through the center beam holes to lockon A, which is positioned on the outer side of the layout. See fig. 5-16. Cut the wires to the necessary length. The two

wires are the main feed lines, and they will power any train around most of the outer loop short of the block sections. Attach the red wire to the no. 1 terminal on the lockon and the

black, or ground, wire to the no. 2 terminal.

Plug in the transformer, turn on the power, and turn up the speed control. The engine should run from one switch around the back of the layout and stop at the switch on the other side. The locomotive will not go any farther because you have placed insulated pins here to create blocks. Either leave the wires attached to lockon A or solder them to the end portion (not the middle) of the rail, as shown in fig. 5-17. Drill holes in the tabletop to route the wires underneath for a neater appearance.

Now you can start "blocking" your layout. For this you'll use the Atlas connectors. Run

another red wire from terminal post no. 16 to the left side of the connector. This is the hot feed to this unit, and this sole wire will be all you need to energize all three blocks on the railroad. The ground for the entire system will be provided by lockon A. Run another piece of red wire from the Atlas connector—first button left—and connect it to the no. 1 terminal of lockon B (fig. 5-16), since this goes to the middle or third rail.

Power up and run the test engine into this part of the main line, which we will call block A. If the switch is off, the engine will stop as soon as it crosses the insulated section. Place the yellow switch in the up position, and the engine should run. If it doesn't, double-check your work so far.

Next, attach the middle Atlas off-on switch to lockon C and the switch farthest to the right to lockon D—the holding track. After testing, you can solder the wires or leave them attached to lockon post no. 1.

With all blocks wired, try to run an engine in all of the blocks. We haven't got to the switches yet, so have your "brakeman" work them manually. You should now be able to run a train into a block, shut it down, bring up another train, and give it a turn on the main line. Once you get the hang of it, you'll be a real railroad operator. The wiring for running trains is now complete (I told you it would be easy), so you can turn your attention to the switches and their operation.

SWITCH MACHINE CONTROL

Route all controller cables to the switches and connect them as described in the instructions. It's pretty straightforward. Three wires go to three terminals! The only problem is the switch machine farthest to the left of the control panel. The controller cable isn't long enough to reach it, so you have to add a bit more. You can accomplish this by running single black wires to each of the three terminals or purchasing a three-wire cable at any hobby shop. Cut, splice, and solder a piece on and you're in business.

Out of the box all Lionel switch machines work on track voltage, but the speed of the throw varies with the power available (the speed control setting). If you slow an engine down to pick up cars in a siding, the switch machine moves slowly or not at all. To compensate for this, go direct to the power supply—in this case the accessory tap—so you can run the switches at a constant voltage for snappy operation.

If you go this route, take the green wire and again go direct to the power source. From the accessory terminal of the RS-1 (fig. 5-15) take this green wire to no. 4 on the terminal strip. Also make a shorter jumper and connect terminal no. 4 to terminal no. 5. This will be the constant voltage tap for the uncoupling tracks.

Run a green wire from no. 4 to each switch machine, hooking it up to the outside plug as shown in fig. 5-18. Keep it mind this plug is to be inserted into the machine only if you are using constant voltage. If you are not, do not place the plug in the unit, since it will disconnect the track voltage, leaving you with a dead switch. Wrap the wire around the plug, tighten the screw, then push it into the switch machine. Check for proper operation. The switch machine lights should be green for the main and red for the diverting route.

If by chance the panel lights on the control do not jibe with the direction the switch machine is thrown, swap the two end wires on the machine to light up the proper colors.

UNCOUPLING TRACKS AND ACCESSORIES

To complete the wiring, all that is left are the uncoupling tracks and the accessories. To wire the uncoupling tracks, use the diagram included in the package. Note that there are four posts on this special section of track. If you want to use track voltage, connect as shown in fig. 5-19 with the tracer wire connected to terminal no. 4.

Again, for snappier operation use constant voltage. Simply hook up wires 1, 2, and 4 as shown in fig. 5-19. The no. 3 wire will go directly to no. 5 on the accessory terminal strip. Place the coupler at either end of a car over the center magnet, turn up the accessory control knob to about the eleven o'clock position, and see what happens. The coupler should spring open. With the exception of the accessories, you now have a fully operational railroad for moving trains, switching, and uncoupling.

The flasher, crossing gate, and rotating beacon are last to install and are perhaps the simplest of all. See figs. 5-20 and 5-21. From terminal no. 1 run a yellow wire directly to the Atlas 205, just as you did with the block controls.

In the case of the flasher and crossing gate, run a yellow wire from the 205 to one side of each item; the wire from the other post will go directly to the insulated track sections.

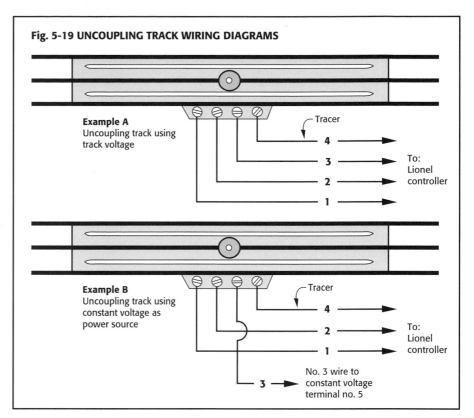

Fig. 5-19 UNCOUPLING TRACK WIRING DIAGRAMS

Example A Uncoupling track using track voltage

Tracer
4
3 → To: Lionel
2   controller
1

Example B Uncoupling track using constant voltage as power source

Tracer
4
2 → To: Lionel
1   controller

3 → No. 3 wire to constant voltage terminal no. 5

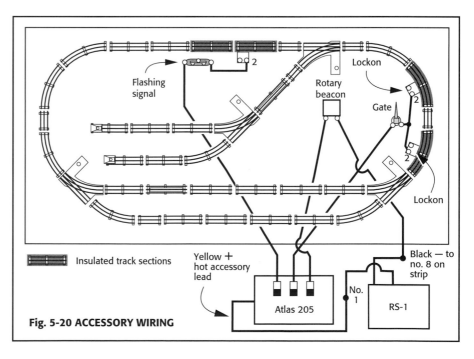

Flashing signal

Rotary beacon

Lockon

Gate

Lockon

Insulated track sections

Yellow + hot accessory lead

Atlas 205

No. 1

RS-1

Black — to no. 8 on strip

Fig. 5-20 ACCESSORY WIRING

In this way the wheels of each passing car will act as a switch, energizing the operating accessory.

You could run power directly to each accessory, but since there will be times when you want to shut them down, I offer the option of doing so with the least expense.

From the 205, run a yellow wire to one side of the flasher,

Fig. 5-21. When using an insulated track to control flashers or crossing gates, the hot lead is run to one terminal (yellow lead—left), with the black lead (right) going to the track. When the train wheels bridge the gap, you have contact and the accessory is activated.

Fig. 5-22. Certain applications require some creative wiring. Here on the crossing gate we use two insulated sections of track, so we also need two sets of wires. On the left is the yellow lead from the transformer, and on the right we continue the circuit to the track (one to each insulated section).

Fig. 5-23. With one hand on the throttle, the other hand can be used to control switches, accessories, and uncoupling of cars. Here the author guides one of his pet GP-38s through a switch while the Southern Pacific diesel waits her turn.

then a black wire from the other side of the flasher to lockon terminal no. 2, located on the insulated track section just before the mountain.

Use black wire as the ground feed, just as you did with the main feed. If everything checks out okay, solder the wire onto the track and move on to the crossing gate. Do not anchor the flasher or the gate permanently at this time, as this will allow you some freedom when you get to the scenery part of layout building.

To operate the crossing gate realistically, you earlier installed two insulated track sections with a half-section of regular track in between to trigger the gate from either end to protect the motorists on your layout. A yellow wire should now be connected from the Atlas 205 to one terminal on the gate itself. From the gate run two black wires, one to each insulated section, to activate the crossing gate. Either solder these wires, as

shown in fig. 5-22, or use the no. 2 terminal on the lockon.

Last is wiring the rotary beacon. This is the easiest, but with a twist that will allow you to control when the beacon operates. Run a yellow wire from the Atlas 205 to one terminal on the bottom of the beacon. See fig. 5-20. Run a black wire back to terminal 8 on the terminal strip. Turn the rotary beacon on by pushing the switch forward, off in the opposite direction.

Now, before we get into the fun part—scenery—go ahead and run your trains, fig. 5-23. This is a good time to check out all of your trackwork, cars, accessories, and wiring to see that everything performs properly, and to correct or fine-tune things when necessary. You may want to test the operating couplers on each car to make sure they open and close properly on the uncoupling sections. Above all, take plenty of time to have fun with the railroad you have created.

CHAPTER SIX

Basic Layout Scenery

Fig. 6-1. Most model railroads include some mountain scenery and a tunnel or two. Our Lionel layout is no exception. This tunnel portal is offered by Mountains in Minutes.

After final testing of your layout to make sure it's properly wired and all accessories work, the last step is building some scenery and installing buildings. This stage of construction will transform your 4' x 8' layout and give your train operations a purpose. While some may shun this fun part of model railroading, if only from lack of experience, both materials and books are available today on the subject that make it enjoyable for even the very beginner. Keep in mind that if you don't care for the desired effect initially achieved, ground cover, grass and related scenery items can be scraped up, changed or redone over and over until you are satisfied. But let's think positive. If you read this chapter, you'll get better than acceptable results the very first time. It's that easy.

SELECTING AND PLACING BUILDINGS

The first step is to select the buildings you'll be using and to place them in their appropriate locations along with operating accessories. For structures, I've picked some

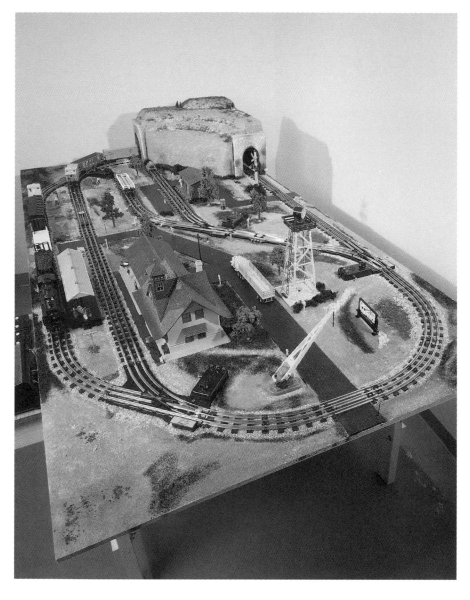

Fig. 6-2. Here's how the layout looks after buildings and scenery are added. Buildings and accessories are identified in fig. 3-2.

that I let it set overnight for a more secure bond.

Lionel kits and most others on the market come already colored; the walls are one color, the windows another, the roof still another. If you elect to change colors—to suit your own railroad colors or motif— the time to think about this is before assembly and not after. Most parts are usually molded together on a sprue, so painting is easy beforehand. To try to paint windows and other smaller details after you cement them into the building is pure torture. In fact, it may turn you off for this phase of the hobby. Remember: Paint first, assemble later.

ROAD CONSTRUCTION

When the buildings are placed to your satisfaction, it's time to begin road construction. Roads can be built in a number of ways. Some folks actually build forms out of ⅛" x ¼" balsa wood and pour plaster into them; that tends to get sloppy, especially around the tracks. Others mix the plaster a little dryer and mold it to conform to their track plan. Some just paint roads on the plywood with flat black paint.

I use plain O gauge roadbed turned upside down. The best way to start is to map the roads out on the table, as shown in fig. 6-3. This roadbed can be curved to a certain degree, but as this is a beginner's guide, I made them straight.

To make roads as realistic as possible, run the roadbed under the tracks as you approach the grade crossings, as shown in fig. 6-3. If there are any wire connections at these points, cut around them. That

from the Lionel catalog. The freight house and Rico station are from kits; the station platform is also a kit but does not need glue as a holding agent. It simply snaps together. The locations of the buildings I selected are shown in fig. 6-2 and were identified back in Chapter Three (fig. 3-2), where the List of Supplies is given. Other kits from Bachmann (the old Plasticville) can also

be used, as can many other varieties available from your railroad specialty shop or local train shows.

Assembling these kits provides hours of enjoyment. Both Lionel kits go together easily using plastic cement. The freight house took only a short time to assemble; the Rico station kit took a little longer because of its unique roof design, which required

Fig. 6-3. Right, top: Roads on your layout can be made very simply by turning standard O gauge roadbed upside down, cutting it, and painting it black. This shows the first cut as you come to an intersection. **Center:** Joining is easy as you lead the road to its next point. **Bottom:** With O gauge track you can lead the road right under the track. Notice how the author placed the road to one side of the track section to allow placement of the ties for added realism.

is the beauty of cork roadbed as a base—it will spring close to the wire for an almost invisible appearance.

After the roads are laid out, cut and placed, mark the edges with a pencil (fig. 6-4), remove the roads, and proceed to lay the glue down. My preference is Elmer's yellow glue because it has less water then the white kind and tends to set up and dry quicker. Just a bit goes a long way. Squeeze the glue down and spread it with one of those foam applicators, as shown in fig. 6-5.

Don't worry about the edges, as the rest of the ground cover will hide any errors. Place some glue on the edges that butt up against each other. And don't be too fussy or too critical about absolute squareness; real roads seldom are square. Besides, we'll be putting a "topcoat" on later, after all is dry. The installed road network is shown in fig. 6-6.

The next step is to coat the roads with joint compound. If you want to skip this step, you can just paint the cork black, and the road will have a texture like a worn blacktop road.

Fig. 6-4. When your roads are laid out the way you want them, mark their location in preparation for gluing.

Fig. 6-5. The cork roads are fastened to the plywood with yellow glue. A little glue goes a long way in holding the cork material down. A foam paint applicator is a handy tool for spreading the yellow glue evenly.

Fig. 6-6. This is how your railroad should look with the roads and accessories in place. Naturally, you have the final say in their location and arrangement. After all, it's your railroad!

However, I recommend using joint compound, since we did some splicing at the corners and ends. The joint compound will add that extra depth we are looking for. All you really need is a small container of joint compound. Take a foam brush and apply a skim coat to the roadbed, as shown in fig. 6-7. Apply just enough to cover the cork. An excessive coating will crack later. On the edges, taper the compound downward to simulate the road's shoulder. Again, don't be too picky applying the compound. When you paint the surface later, it will all come together.

Fig. 6-7. For the final road surface, the author used a very light brushing of joint compound over the cork. You could also use a textured paint if you have some around.

ADDING TRACK TIES

While the roads are setting, the next step is the placement of additional ties under each track section. Obviously, you don't have to do this, but to me this is what really starts to make your railroad look realistic. Fig. 6-8 shows the difference between track as it comes and track with the extra ties installed. If you place four additional ties to an O gauge section (good), you'll need about 132 ties. If you place six ties to a section (better), as I did, make up about 200.

You can make extra ties by purchasing ¼" x ½" stripwood and cutting it in 2¼" lengths. Stain them black or dark brown and spread them out on newspaper to dry.

A far better approach is just to purchase a bag of ties from Moondog Express (104 W. Ocean Ave., Lompoc, CA 93436). They are made of rubber and fit snugly under each track section. When you start to place them, loosen up the track a bit, insert the ties, and

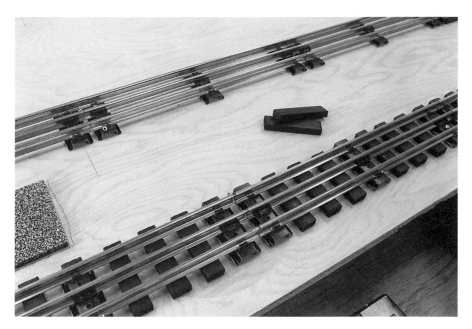

Fig. 6-8. With this layout, you have a choice. Here the author illustrates the track with ties (bottom) and without (top). Either way, ballasting the track will improve the appearance.

retighten everything. Gluing is not necessary. In size, these ties are about ⅟₃₂ of an inch higher then the space under the track, so as you tighten the track back down, you exert pressure on the ties, and they in turn remain snug. Later we'll apply ballast.

MAKING A MOUNTAIN

No layout would ever be complete without at least one mountain with a tunnel, and ours will not be the exception. They are fun to make and add yet another dimension to a model railroad. Our mountain will be removable, so it can be

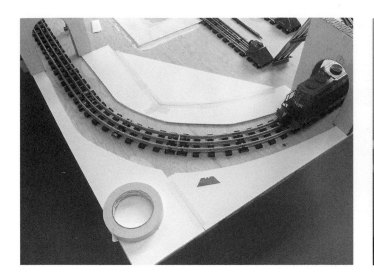

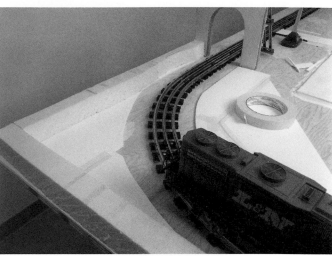

Fig. 6-9. This is the start of the mountain. Use foam core for the base, with the portals attached at the ends. Be sure to leave enough material to work with on the outboard side of the mountain—that is, toward the inner part of the layout.

Fig. 6-10. The next step is to build a foundation, using strips of polystyrene insulation about 1½" wide. Keep checking clearances of your longest and largest pieces of rolling stock as construction progresses. Corrections are more difficult to make later on.

easily stored if you put the trains away after the holidays.

Set up the tunnel portals again in their pre-marked spots. The first thing to do now is to build a foam core foundation. This is a material that frame shops and photographic equipment stores sell for mounting prints or photographs. You can also find foam core at craft centers. Foam core is light, easy to cut and work with, and stable under most normal conditions.

Cut four strips about 6" x 36" long. Lay these down even with the end of the table, lining up the front edge with the tunnel portal. Cut the outer radius so the curved track clears the foam core, as shown in fig. 6-9. Don't worry about being perfect, as this will be inside the tunnel and will be our first base line. Do the same for the inside of the track, as shown in the photographs. When you get something pleasing in shape, stop and tape everything together. Keep in

mind that if by chance the foam core overlaps the scenic material, it can be cut back and hidden by the ground cover later. With these basics down, the fun begins.

Go to the lumberyard and purchase two sheets of 2' x 8' extruded polystyrene insulation. At my lumberyard I could get it in a thickness of either 1½" or 2". My pick is the 1½". To me it's just easier to cut and work with, especially when cutting curves. The first few pieces will be narrow in width as we start upward. Here, in these tight situations, the thinner insulation just works better.

For cutting implements, you can use a hacksaw or small crosscut saw or even an old serrated bread knife. Set up a table to work on, keep the vacuum handy for cleanup, and you're ready to begin.

Cut a few 1¼"-wide strips to go against the edge of the table, as shown in fig. 6-10. Make sure the tunnel portal

rests square against the end, as we'll glue both of these items into position. Now is the time to make clearance cuts for the engine inside the tunnel itself. As you work, keep checking clearances both outside and inside with your largest and longest engine or cars. Once you start to finalize the mountain in rough terms it will be virtually impossible to pull these pieces apart without ruining all your work.

Start building on the inside of the curve, being overly generous towards the very outside, or the side that faces the center of the plywood. Later, when all is set, you'll start to carve a reasonable facsimile of a mountain, so any additional material here is just more to work with. Again, as you go along, keep checking those clearances, especially on the outside of the curve and the portals. Start to eye up the squareness of the portals as you move along. Using Elmer's glue, stack up two or three layers, place weights on top, then let everything dry 24 hours. (For quicker assembly, use latex contact cement.)

In the next session, continue to build upward with the side pieces until you (1) clear the rolling stock and (2) are able to start laying complete sheets across the top. See fig. 6-11. As you position the uppermost pieces, start a gradual taper near the top of the mountain. A look at any photo or real-life landscape can give you a better understanding if you have any doubts. Let your creative juices flow here.

For subsequent work I recommend you move the mountain from your layout to a work table (fig. 6-12) for final assembly, shaping, painting and scenery details. As soon as you have piled up five or six layers, stop and let everything dry at least 12 hours or more.

The next phase will be to shape what you have now in order to get a better picture of how to continue the upward spiral. Take your saw blade or Stanley Surfoam blade and work on the front section until you get a pleasing slope upward, as shown in fig. 6-13. When you're satisfied, stop. Keep in mind that if you take too much off, you'll have a hard time replacing material.

Finish by placing full layers on top to a height of around 14" to 15". If your layout is in a corner, or you are trying to hide the water meter, a column, or some other unnatural fixture in your house, you could go higher and gradually taper the mountain to blend with the landscape. Additional work with a file and handsaw will finish the shaping.

Fig. 6-11. Now build the foam layers upward. With more levels, the mountain is taking shape and the structure is becoming sturdier.

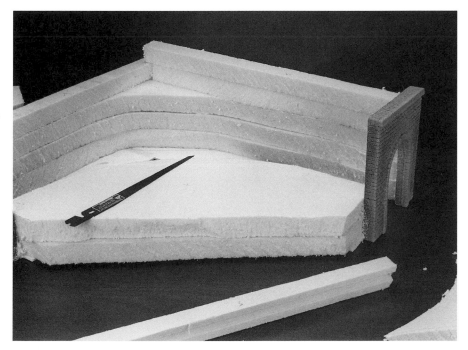

Fig. 6-12. Move the mountain to a workbench and keep working upward with narrow strips until you reach a height where full pieces can be used.

To scenic your prize, first go over the mountain with your hand, wiping it clean of all small debris that would possibly stick to a paintbrush. Set up an area where you can make a mess without the fear of destroying something.

Fig. 6-13. As you progress, you might want to work on the front side, in order to get a better idea of the slope. Here the author uses a fine blade to shape the foam to make it look like a mountain.

Fig. 6-14. Because of the rough texture it's best to pour the paint on the mountain. Pour a little on, then spread it with a brush.

Fig. 6-15. Sprinkle ground foam onto the wet paint. Note how the vertical marks on the front of the mountain add to the realism of the rock.

Spread out a drop cloth or a layer of heavy brown kraft or newspaper, and you're ready to start painting.

When doing scenery on a small layout, try to stick to lighter browns and other earth tones. The lighter the color, the bigger a confined area seems to be. Another plus is that when you start to apply grass, ground cover or "dirt," the lighter color seems to accent these important ingredients rather than conceal them.

My neighborhood hardware store handles Pittsburgh paints, and without much effort a quart of "Brownstone" was whipped up for this purpose. Whatever is left from the mountain will be used on the flatter surfaces of the layout later.

Ask members of the family not to bother you for a good hour. Since the rough foam is a bear to paint by brush, tip the can and literally pour the paint on, as shown in fig. 6-14. This not only gives a thicker coat, but adds texture as you start to spread ground cover.

If you've never done any scenery texturing before, the drill goes like this:
• Pour out some paint and spread it with a brush.
• When you have covered a good-sized area, sprinkle on ground cover, as shown in fig. 6-15. I use Woodland Scenics "dirt" and "grass" ground foam. Woodland Scenics "coarse turf" in dark green (T65) and yellow (T61) placed into cracks (fig. 6-16) add life, while grass and dirt just add that third dimension needed on your mountain. My particular mountain has a flat area on the top, since I intend to move the rotary beacon

to this location later. In my neck of the woods, I notice that flatter areas seem to grow grass more easily, while rocky vertical planes harbor dirt rather than vegetation.

• Work downward, pouring the paint on and sprinkling on ground foam. As you progress downward, change from grass cover to more and more dirt. If you look closely, you'll see that the Surfoam blade did an excellent job of marking the foam in a way that would take Mother Nature years. Horizontal lines from the layers only add interest. They will remind you of the rock strata visible along many an interstate highway.

• Keep working on the project as the paint starts to thicken and dry. Any fine material like grass or dirt will sink in and blend with the paint. Add color and texture until the paint will take no more and the color remains constant. At this point you will start to notice how really good you are at landscaping.

• As you get down towards the bottom, sprinkle on some coarse ballast. In real life heavy rocks and related material roll down from the effects of gravity.

• Whatever you do, don't overdo the scenic effects on the mountain. When you think you have reached one plateau of application, stop, step back and view your accomplishments. You can always add more grass or ground cover while the paint is still wet. Believe me, it's hard to take it away. When you are satisfied with your results, put the mountain aside to dry while you turn your attention to the track ballasting.

Fig. 6-16. Placing Woodland Scenics yellow and green ground foam in nooks and crannies will add depth to your work.

BALLASTING THE TRACK

Whether you choose to add additional ties or not, the addition of ballast to the track makes a big difference in the appearance of the railroad. I use Highball Products ballast, which is available in hobby shops in various grades and colors. It's made from genuine limestone. I've also used parakeet cage gravel for ballast, and I've even heard of some who have used kitty litter.

There are numerous ways to ballast track. If your pike is permanent, you could just pour the ballast down between the ties and let it lie loose. If you're going to move the railroad or store it on edge, you'll want to fix the ballast in place.

A diluted solution of Elmer's white glue mixed about three parts water to one part glue (with a drop of two of liquid detergent to make the water wetter) makes an excellent bonding solution. You can also use a commercial product marketed by Woodland Scenics called "Scenic Cement." When sprayed on, it bonds the ballast to the plywood and to individual ties.

To start, dump three to four boxes of the ballast into a box. Grab a small dixie cup and scoop some up. Spread this ballast down between the rails and around the ties, both inside and outside. Take a small paintbrush and clean up around the outside of the tracks to a uniform depth of ½" or so, as shown in fig. 6-17. Doing this makes a neat "right-of-way," as seen on most of today's modern railroads.

For variety I like to use a lighter limestone ballast on the main line, and a darker, cinder type on sidings or rails with less traffic. It is more realistic and adds depth to little-used (or little-maintained) trackage. If you want, you can totally bury the ties on the sidings to further the effect.

I like to work an area of about a foot at a time, but there is nothing wrong with

Fig. 6-17. Left, top: To start ballasting the track, pour some ballast into a paper cup and spread it around and between the ties. Center: The next step is to spread it evenly with a brush while cleaning off the ties. Keep the edges within about ½" to ¾" of the ties. Bottom: The final step is to lock everything down with the scenic cement from Woodland Scenics. After spraying, clean the track by wiping with a cloth.

laying the ballast down on the entire railroad, then going back and securing it all down. Whatever you do, don't do the inside of the switches, because ballast can work its way into the mechanism, leading to trouble down the line. Ballasting the outside of the machines is okay, but again, keep the points clear of both ballast and glue or cement.

As you fix the ballast in place, wipe the cement off the rails as much as possible without disturbing the ballast underneath. Go back a short time later and wipe any glue or cement off the tops of the ties. Wipe again, if necessary. Diluted glue dries slowly, so when you've finished, let the ballast dry overnight.

I mentioned that you can bury the ties on sidings in ballast. Give it a try on one of your sidings. Don't brush the ties clean of cinder ballast. A pinch of grass or ground cover applied between the ties and before the glue is applied will make these tracks look just that much older and neglected.

PAINTING THE ROADS

Painting the roads is next. I suggest using a semi-gloss

black paint and applying it with a coarse (read "inexpensive") brush. This will give your roads a nice textured surface. As you paint around the curves, let the brush go around the bend, not straight through. This makes a traffic or wear pattern for added realism.

Finish off the grade crossing, using an artist's brush. Work carefully, so you don't get any paint on the rails.

Paint out from the edges of the road surface about ½", so the scenic material can blend right up to it without any white joint compound showing. My painted roads are shown in fig. 6-18.

PLANTING TREES

Tree planting is next. You have many alternatives. In my younger days I used to spend weeks in the summer on my uncle's farm. There I would collect various weeds, spray them green or brown, and turn out some very acceptable trees. I also picked younger bottom branches from trees and glued lichen to them, again creating reasonable facsimiles. Today there are many brands of commercial trees available at your local hobby shop that are better than any I could produce.

So my choice here was Woodland Scenics trees in heights from 3 to 6 or 7 inches. One good thing about these trees is that they come with detachable bases. So before you paint a base coat, spot the trees where you want them, separate the trees from their bases, and glue the bases down. Now apply the brown base coat right over the bases, making everything that much more true to life. Another ad-

Fig. 6-18. With the mountain complete, the roads painted, trees in and ballast all done, it's time to complete the project.

vantage to these trees is that you can pull them off when storing the layout.

SIGNS

If you intend to place small signs, roadside traffic warnings, or anything else with a cast-on base, now is the time to do it. Lionel's roadside series (2180) is excellent for this, as is Life-Like's series, which also includes such nifty items as telephone booths, trackside relay boxes and related details like station accessories and people. They are all very inex-

pensive and add life to your railroad—and with just a dab of Elmer's glue on each base, they will stay fastened until you are ready to redo or change your pike.

FINISHING TOUCHES

Now you're ready to texture the rest of the layout. If you had fun with the mountain, this will be a piece of cake. In addition to the brown latex paint, a brush or two, and a rag (just in case), you'll need some additional Woodland Scenics products. A bag of

Fig. 6-19. Using a paintbrush, the author finishes the scenery. By dabbing the brush, you can increase the amount of paint, providing some "tooth" for applying grass or other scenic products. Don't worry if scenic material gets on the roads. You can clean it up later.

tinctive part to play. It is the bonding agent for the scenic materials. Don't pour it on, as you did on the mountain. Instead, take a good brush full, spread it down, then dab the brush up and down (fig. 6-19) to give the paint some "tooth." This roughness will help to grab the turf, grass or earth ground foam materials. Sprinkle on the ground cover mix from the paper cup. Apply paint along the base of the ballast, too.

Do a section at a time, so the paint does not have a chance to set up before you apply the scenic blend. If you run into a particular spot on your pike where you may need some heavier ground cover, apply the paint more thickly, then press the lichen or ground cover into it for a secure bond. When you come to your tree bases, paint them also. Then sprinkle on some grass or dirt to blend them into the surrounding terrain. You want the paint to be wet as you work. Believe me, everything will stick much better that way.

Think of the photos of my layout as only a guide. Try not to copy too much of it directly, because your own ideas should show on your layout.

Three of the four corners have been left bare for future expansion. Perhaps you may want to add a Lionel accessory like the operating switch tower where the gate is, operated from the same insulated track sections, to give more action at this end of the layout. All in all, ideas for improving a layout and the application of them are endless.

I suggest that you just mark and paint the areas

earth turf (T42) and perhaps a bag or two of coarse turf in different colors, plus some "dirt" and lichen, will put you in a good position to landscape your layout in grand style. For easy application, place a small quantity of dirt, grass, gravel and earth turf in a paper cup. Heavier turf will be applied by fingertip. A pinch of coarser material here and there will be fine as you move along.

All you have to remember is what things look like in real life. If you need a review, take a walk near a railroad, in an industrial area, or even in your very own backyard. In little-used areas, grass or weeds will grow. In well-used areas more earth will show, denoting traffic or wear. You can model both, and as you progress you'll see what I mean.

Dab a moderately heavy coat of paint on the plywood, taking into account that the plywood will absorb more than its share. The paint has a dis-

Fig. 6-20. This scene on the finished layout shows some of the hundreds of details you can add to this 4' x 8' model railroad. You can have lots of fun placing figures in believable combinations like the two workmen in the foreground.

where buildings, accessories, or the tunnel are to be placed. Don't texture them. Everything will sit a bit more evenly if it is not rocking on turf or lichen. If you want to change things around at a later time, you can always go back, spread some additional paint or white glue, and scenic that particular area again. The important thing is to take your time, even if it means doing an area of only about one square foot at a time. The more detail (and attention) you give to a spot, the better it will look. Apply some ground cover, step back and look at the effect, and then add some more if you like.

After the initial ground cover is done, can you add anything else? You bet. In reality, you have just begun.

Placing people around the pike, as in fig. 6-20, adds an immeasurable amount of reality to your station platforms, streets, and work areas. Life-Like has an excellent selection of figures in all shapes, sizes, and positions, including kids, street workers, baggage handlers, conductors and other action type figures. A number of other manufacturers also provide excellent O scale figures. For ease of standing, most figures come with a molded-on plastic base. For even more realism, however, cut these bases off and glue the figures down permanently.

Trailer trucks from Lionel and cars from aftermarket sources can be placed on the roads. If you see some of the older Dinky toys at flea markets, grab them up. They are perfect for Lionel layouts.

You can add some lichen around the switch machines to hide those wires, around that base line on the mountain, and in front of buildings to simulate evergreens.

Foot paths can be made with lighter colored sand. Mailboxes, telephone poles, trackside relay boxes and other details can add dimension to your pike.

I could go on and on, but I think it's time for your imagination to take over. After all, that's the fun part.

CHAPTER SEVEN

Maintenance and Basic Troubleshooting

Fig. 7-1. Here's a modest maintenance kit that includes lubricants, tools, and rags, plus some cleaners that require a little explanation. The Sheila Shine is used for stainless parts on accessories like milk or cattle platforms. RemAction Scrubber is good for cleaning up older Lionel trains. The can of compressed air is for drying parts quickly, and the cream wax brings back the shine on older equipment after cleaning.

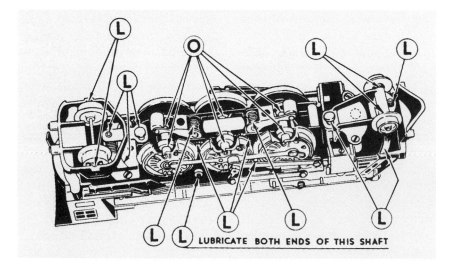

Fig. 7-2. Most Lionel maintenance sheets contain some kind of line drawing like this one to show you where to lubricate your prized steam locomotives properly. File maintenance information for future reference.

Routine or preventive maintenance of your Lionel trains requires little mechanical knowledge. All new engines, cars, and accessories include basic instructions on their care, but let's reinforce these with some additional detailed information.

EQUIPMENT MAINTENANCE

Chances are that you will be pulling the chief maintenance duties on your railroad, so you'll want to have a small lube and repair kit ready. See fig. 7-1. Common, everyday tools like screwdrivers, pliers, diagonal-cutting pliers, etc., will work well for most of the maintenance chores you'll be doing. Lionel is good at making its powered units easily accessible for repairs. Smaller, so-called jeweler's screwdriver sets are available at hobby shops for those small screws in tight places. I also suggest you pick up a small needle-nosed crimping and cutting pliers at your local hobby shop.

For testing circuits a good voltmeter is a must, as well as a pair of 3-foot test leads and four medium-sized alligator clips. You may even want to add a used transformer to your workbench for testing the equipment. To finish your tool kit, I'd throw in a pencil-type soldering iron, resin-core (never acid-core) solder, and a

Dremel power tool for finish work or light polishing. If a problem requires more specialized tools, forget the repair and take the locomotive, car, or accessory to an authorized Lionel Service Station.

Steam locomotives. The basic thing to know—whether you're maintaining an old, postwar Lionel or a brand new engine—is that a grease-type lubricant should be applied to all exposed moving parts. This includes all gears and truck pivots, as well as those spring contacts that pick up the electrical current. See fig. 7-2. Oil should be applied to axles or on the bearings associated with the main drivers.

Older steam locomotives with smoke units usually have a buildup in the stack from the pellets used to make the smoke. This buildup can be cleaned out with a Q-Tip. See fig. 7-3.

Diesels. Diesels are easier to maintain than steam locomotives because there are few-

Fig. 7-3. Some older engines are not difficult to maintain. For instance, to change the front light bulb, remove the screw just behind the feedwater heater and in front of the stack. The white residue around the stack is from smoke pellets. A Q-Tip can be used to wipe that away quickly. Finally, the lockout switch for the "E" unit is that chrome swinging lever just in front of the bell.

er moving parts. If you flip a late model Lionel diesel over, you'll note gears on the bottom attached to a motor mounted crosswise on the truck. A drop of oil applied with a toothpick at the end of the axles will suffice. A minute amount of lubricant is all that's required on the gears. See fig. 7-4. Excessive lubrication, fig. 7-5, is just as bad as none at all. Too

Fig. 7-4. Newer Lionel diesels are relatively maintenance-free. Just an occasional touch of lubricant on the gears that run along the top of the truck is all that's really needed to keep your equipment running.

Fig. 7-5. Too much lubricant is just as bad as no lubricant. This is an example of overdoing it. Once that lubricant starts to fly onto the wheels, spoiling electrical contact and picking up lint, the fun is over.

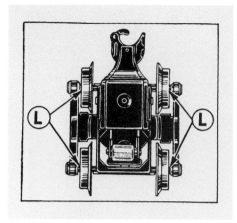

Fig. 7-6. On freight or passenger cars, the lubrication job is easy. Just a drop of very light oil is all you need to keep those cars rolling.

Fig. 7-7. Manufacturers like LaBelle and Lionel make light oils for your accessories. Here the author is doing periodic maintenance on an older accessory, the 397 Coal Loader.

much oil or grease will attract dust to the wheels, spoiling electrical contact and possibly fouling the motor, brushes, and commutator.

A good habit to develop is to turn the engine over on a pad, lubricate it, and then run it by applying power from a pair of test leads connected to a transformer. Hook one alligator clip to the contact roller, and the other to the locomotive frame. Turn up the power and let the engine run a few minutes. It's better to have any excess lube fly off during this bench test than later onto your track or switches.

Other Lionel engines (Collector Series) like the GGls, PAs, or F3 diesels have different motors or gearing arrangements, so you'll want to study the specific maintenance procedures in their instructions.

Cars. Freight or passenger car trucks are by far the easiest to maintain. As shown in fig. 7-6, a drop of oil at those four points will keep your rolling stock in good shape for at least a year, depending of course on usage.

Older cars purchased at train meets are easy to clean up. They can be taken apart by separating the body from the chassis, placed in a bath of lukewarm water and Joy dishwashing detergent, and scrubbed clean. A bit of wax like Midway-Boyle's Old English, applied sparingly, will bring back the shine.

Accessories. Accessories, too, need tender loving care. Maintenance instructions are packed with new accessories. However, if you pick up one or two of the 1950s vintage operating accessories, a few tips are in order. First, if you have to get inside an old accessory, work slowly. Some covers are held on by metal tabs; over they years, they have probably been bent back or forth more then once or twice and are subject to breakage. Moving parts deserve special care. Solenoids can be stiff; they may need a prod or a push to get going. Vibrators may need adjustment. Bulbs can be replaced easily. Sometimes just a touch of light train oil can work wonders. See fig. 7-7.

Some of the very best oils—aside from "railroad" oils such as the LaBelle brand—can be found in gun shops. Remington Arms makes some of the best light oils in the world, which contain a hint of Teflon for extra lubricating power. If gun collectors trust this oil with their multi-thousand-dollar rifles or shotguns, our Lionel trains can benefit from this product, also. Another firearm lubricant is called Gunslick, fig. 7-8. It is an anhydrous graphite—simply meaning there is no water in its makeup. Again, don't overdo it.

TRACK MAINTENANCE

Track also needs periodic attention. When you are laying new track, and periodically thereafter, check all pin connections, paying close attention to the insulating pins. If your layout becomes permanent and quite large, consider soldering the track together at the joints for extra durability and increased electrical reliability.

Switches are relatively maintenance-free; all they

Fig. 7-8. The author has found that Gunslick, a premium lubricant sold in gun shops, is ideal for Lionel cars and accessories.

Fig. 7-9. Switches are easy to keep clean. A wipe with an inexpensive paintbrush will rid these units of dirt, "grass," or other debris.

need is a casual brushing now and then to rid the points of unwanted turf or ballast that may have gotten there by the constant motion of your rolling stock. An inexpensive paint brush is fine for this, as shown in fig. 7-9.

Even in the cleanest of areas dust accumulates on the track surface, eventually causing a film to build up on the wheels, track, or both. Occasionally clean the track with a rag wet with one of the liquid track cleaners sold in hobby shops. See fig. 7-10.

The maintenance of Lionel equipment on your railroad will not be a time-consuming process, by any means. Lionel trains are built tough—just look at the Lionel equipment still around from the early 1900s. So take care of them now on a somewhat regular basis, and you'll be able to enjoy them for a long time.

BASIC TROUBLESHOOTING TIPS

(COURTESY LIONEL TRAINS, INC.)

No lights or operation. Make sure the transformer is plugged in. Try a lamp or other device (radio, clock) to make sure power is available at the outlet. Also try the transformer's circuit breaker.

Circuit breaker trips immediately upon application of power. Recheck wiring while looking for short circuits. Disconnect all wiring if possible. Then reconnect the wires one at a time until the defective circuit is found.

Train runs, but horn/whistle or direction buttons will not work. Check track connections to transformer. Horn/whistle or bell and direction work only on the track output terminals.

No change when direction button is pressed. Make sure locomotive reversing unit is not locked out.

No operation or intermittent operation of accessories. Make sure adjusted accessory output voltage is high enough to operate accessory. Also, check for loose, shorted, or improper connections in wiring.

Locomotive runs slowly, or lights dim, at the far end of the track. On some larger layouts, the additional track resistance causes a voltage drop along the track. The solution is to add additional power feeders (via lockons) to the remote areas of your layout.

Intermittent operation with constant tripping of the circuit breaker. Transformer capacity may have been exceeded. Disconnect accessories one at a time until the problem disappears. Check for shorts on the track like paper clips, tinsel, or missing insulation on the inner rail.

Bell button blows the whistle. Check all track wire connections. At the terminal strip, black terminal strip connections are common and should be connected to the common (or outside) rails.

Fig. 7-10. Track cleaning is easy. The author uses a few drops of commercial track cleaner on a rag to pick up accumulated dirt.

CHAPTER EIGHT

Operating Accessories

I've always loved Lionel's operating accessories. The popular ones come to mind immediately. The coal elevator that I first noticed in the hardware store when I was a boy was finally added to my collection almost thirty years later. Coal was big business on all Lionel Lines, as witnessed by the sheer number of coal cars available to go with such notables as the 397 (model number) Coal Loader, 456 Coal Ramp and newer 497 Coaling Station. Other commodities? Sure. How about lumber? Here we had a choice. The classic 164 Log Loader, eventually discontinued, was followed by the more horizontal 364 Lumber Conveyor. Even barrels were represented by a vibrating platform Lionel called the 362 Operating Barrel Loader. Add such goodies as switch towers, operating stations, cattle and milk cars, and you have a wonderful list that seems almost endless.

Accessories add so much action and enjoyment to the operation of a layout. They give a

Bascule bridge. One of the classic operating accessories, it combined the operation of the train with the motion of a lift bridge. Back in the 1940s, Lionel termed it "one of the most popular accessories ever manufactured." It's easy to understand why. By pressing a button, you start the bridge moving upward. When a train approaches the bridge, it stops, waits until the bridge returns to its down position, and then proceeds across. This accessory, although too large for a 4' x 8' layout, is one of the author's favorites.

railroad a sense of purpose, generate traffic, and add excitement. Over its many years, Lionel has produced hundreds of operating and non-operating accessories. Many of the older accessories are no longer produced. However, you can find used ones (some forty years old or older) in good operating condition at train shows or swap meets.

I've already suggested a few for your layout, but I want to give you a least a glimpse of the wide variety of accessories that are available. So I'm going to show you a few that I really like. I hope this chapter will whet your appetite for more accessories so that you'll investigate this subject further and pick some additional ones for your layout.

Coal elevator. This has always been a popular accessory, probably because it literally stood above the rest, towering a full 12" tall. Coal was dumped from a dump car (inset photo) into the bin at the bottom and lifted into the tower. It was then dispensed into waiting cars from a chute to the right. The loaded cars would eventually find their way back to be unloaded into the bucket, and the cycle would go on and on.

Gantry crane. This accessory brings hours of operating fun to any layout. The crane rotates a full 360 degrees, the block and tackle with electromagnet can be raised and lowered, and the magnet itself can be activated and turned off—all by remote control. The crane can straddle an industrial siding on your layout, thereby conserving valuable layout real estate. This was a very popular accessory during Lionel's postwar period (it was called a magnet crane back then), and it has been reissued by Lionel Trains, Inc. The latest version features an improved motor and gear system.

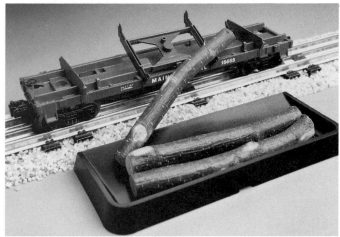

Log loader. Log cars deposit wood logs on one side of this unit. At the press of a button the logs are then lifted up and over the chain-driven conveyor into a holding bin on the far side. They can then be loaded onto other dump cars, such as the one pictured at right.

Switch tower. When this accessory is activated by an approaching train, the trainman on the outside platform goes inside the building while the one at the top of the stairs runs down to greet the train. The figures are supposed to give the effect of being the same man. You can find used switch towers at most train meets at reasonable prices.

Forklift loader station. The forklift moves back and forth, simulating the loading of pipes from the Lionel Pipe Co. into freight cars.

Signal bridge. This bridge spans two tracks. It includes dual-facing red and green signals, which are activated by a trackside connector or insulated track section.

Steam clean, wheel grind shop. Typical of the new breed of Lionel accessories are these modular units, which can be grouped together as shown or split apart if space permits. When the wheel grinder is operating, sparks from lighter flints can be seen. The vertical rollers of the washer spin. (Like the bascule bridge, this accessory is too large for a 4' x 8' layout.)

Gooseneck street lamps and illuminated station. When the room lights dim, Lionel layouts bask in the glow of street lamps, signal lights, illuminated buildings, and a variety of other lighted accessories. These old-style gooseneck street lamps come two to a package. Street lamps are also available in more modern styles. The illuminated station is suited to either freight yards or passenger depots. It comes fully assembled.

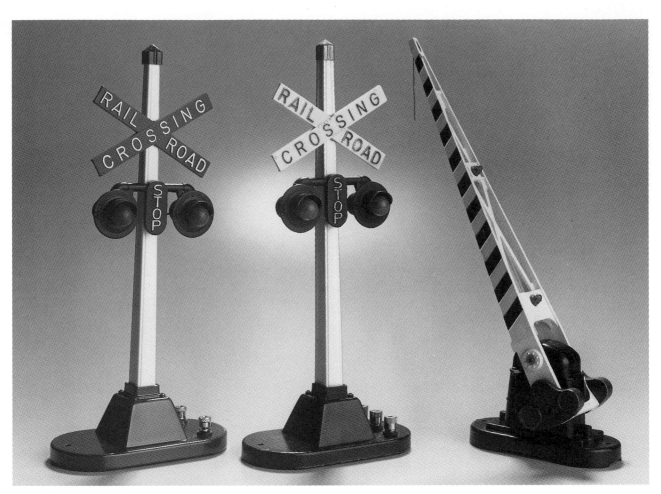

Various signals. Operating signals of various types have been offered by Lionel. Left to right in top photo, older version of grade crossing signal, new version, and grade crossing gate. Bottom photo shows a block signal and semaphore signal.

Searchlight cars. On some models the searchlight will rotate continuously as long as current is applied to the tracks. This rotating beacon creates a dramatic effect during night operation.

Fire car. Youngsters love to play with this car. The ladder can be extended, using a crank on the side of the car.

TV car. When the car is in motion, the cameraman moves around in a circle. The bank of floodlights can be moved manually.

Telephone poles. Small details add dimension to a layout and enhance the realism. Don't overlook such common-place items as telephone poles, which are seen along railroad tracks nationwide. This assortment from Lionel Trains, Inc., includes ten poles with removable bases.

Fueling station and forklift loader station. These two operating accessories from Lionel simulate real-life railroading activities. The attendant at the fueling station in the foreground will, at the push of a button, see to it that your diesel fleet is kept topped off. Workers at the forklift loader station provide loads of pipe for points on down the line.

CHAPTER NINE

What's Next?

Fig. 9-1. When detailing your layout, try to re-create mini scenes like this one. The two workmen appear to have a project going that involves some serious changes to the signal box.

Building a small layout like the one I've described in this book can be the beginning of a lifelong hobby. Exploring new or different avenues of this hobby is fun. You are indeed fortunate that in model railroading there are enough different things to do to keep you interested for many years. In this concluding chapter I'll suggest some areas of this hobby you may want to explore.

DETAILING

One of the first things you can consider doing is adding detail to the layout you've just built. I find this aspect of the hobby very enjoyable. Detailing involves adding people, vehicles, animals, electric and telephone poles, signs, debris, etc. You can spend many enjoyable hours adding the little extras that improve the overall appearance of the layout.

When you position figures, try to create mini-scenes that tell a story. In fig. 9-1 two workmen are doing some repair work near a signal box. You could place these figures so they appear to be talking to each other. You could even set up a scene with a police car pulling up to a curb while a masked man flees down the street. I think you get the general idea.

Fig. 9-2. Station platforms can never have enough people standing around waiting for the next train. Place some figures in family groups with their luggage.

Speaking of figures, even a small layout can use a lot of them. Station platforms, fig. 9-2, can use quite a few people waiting for the next train.

Need some ideas for detailing? Just look around the world you live in. Take a camera and explore some industrial areas (with permission, of course). If there are railroad facilities in your area that you can photograph from public property, take some photos to use for reference when detailing your layout.

SELECTING A NAME

As you become a more advanced model railroader, you'll want to select a name for your empire. You can make up a name that sounds like a real railroad, such as the Midville & Western RR, New England Northern, the Southwest Lines, or Springfield Southern. Right off the bat, these names ring with the importance of the areas they serve.

Or you can come up with something a little corny, like NoMoney & NoAmbition, Choo-Choo Central, or the Alan, Barry and Charlie Lines. A name like this is cute, but you'd probably tire of it quickly.

Another possibility is using a real railroad's name, like Santa Fe, Great Northern, Southern Pacific, Norfolk Southern, Union Pacific, Conrail, etc. This approach has the added advantage that you can select factory-painted locomotives and cars that match your name.

ADDING EQUIPMENT

New models of engines and cars are always coming out of the Lionel plant. This gives you reason to visit your local hobby shop frequently to see what's new. Some folks spend fortunes on trains by buying every new model in sight. This is fine if you have the money, but there's no need to go to this extreme. If you miss a new

Fig. 9-3. For variety on your layout, other manufacturers like Weaver make engines and cars that run on Lionel track with no problems. This is their C-630 diesel in Union Pacific markings.

Fig. 9-4. Heavy-duty switch engines, like this one from K-Line, add greater pulling power in yards or long industrial sidings.

model that you really want at the time of introduction, fear not—you'll probably be able to find a good used one later at a local or national train show.

In addition to Lionel's production, many fine O gauge models are offered by K-Line, Weaver, Williams, Right-Of-Way Industries, and other companies. See figs. 9-3 and 9-4. Engines from Weaver or Williams are made of brass, run smoothly, and have outstanding paint jobs. K-Line puts out some pretty fancy scale-length passenger cars, fig. 9-5, that need wider curves (O54 or O72); they are worth looking into. When you combine wider-radius curves with

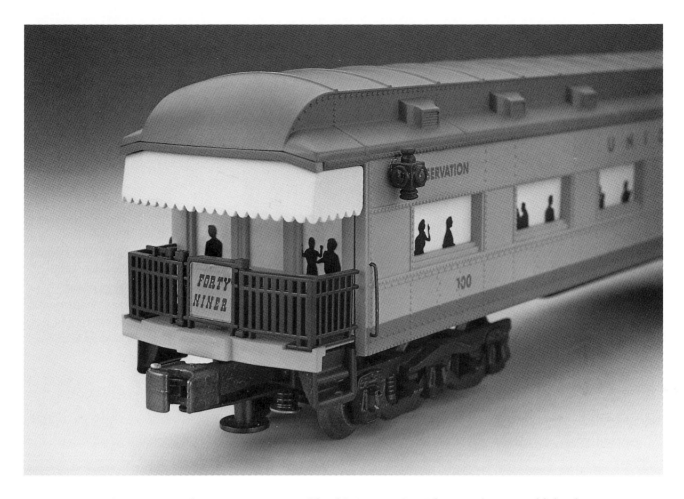

Fig. 9-5. Extra-fancy passenger cars like this "Forty-Niner" from K-Line can add depth to your passenger fleet. For even more realism, people can be placed on that observation platform.

O72 switches, you are really getting into model railroading.

COLLECTING

Collecting Lionel trains is one of the most popular of all aspects of this hobby. Since Lionel has been around since 1900, the list of collectibles is mind-boggling! Some people collect the older Standard gauge, some prefer the prewar era, while others (like me) dwell on the postwar era. Even newer Lionel trains—those produced since 1970—often become collectible, and a growing number of hobbyists specialize in this area. Finding prime examples of older Lionel production in new or like-new condition is a real challenge, especially with prices skyrocketing every year. But again, that's the fun of it.

If you join the TCA (Train Collectors of America), you can attend regional as well as national meets that they host. In my New England area there can be three or more meets a year for Lionel fans. Here people gather their wares, set them up on a table, and sell them for a profit, so they can buy and sell more. Our local meets offer over 200 tables full of Lionel equipment for sale!

If you do get into collecting, one thing to be aware of is the existence of restored units of past Lionel stock. They are okay if marked as such. With the prices so-called "original," "mint," or "like-new" are going for, sometimes a restored unit can make the difference between having a particular model or going without. A trip to a few train shows will open your eyes to what is available and what to pay for it.

It's helpful to purchase collector price guides for the era you're collecting. Greenberg Books is a leader in this department with "guides" for just about any era you pursue.

Beware of those misguided individuals who seem to be lurking in every hobby or form of recreation, trying to make a fast buck. If in doubt about a

Fig. 9-6. Left: Jerry Blaine has a large collection of Lionel, American Flyer, and Ives Standard Gauge trains, as well as Lionel O gauge trains, shown beautifully displayed here. Collecting Lionel and other toy trains can become a hobby unto itself. Photo by George Hall.

Fig. 9-7. Below: David Dansky also has a large collection, beautifully displayed, plus a large layout where he runs Lionel and American Flyer trains in standard, O, and S gauges. Photo by George Hall.

Fig. 9-8. Stan Roy has built a large three-level Lionel layout with beautiful scenery and flawless automatic operation. Using a relay logic system he designed, he can operate thirty-two trains simultaneously. Photo by Chris Becker.

purchase, contact someone from the TCA or ask fellow model railroaders for advice. For the most part, model railroaders are a friendly lot, eager to help out.

As your collection grows, you'll need some space to show it off. Collections go from simple wall displays to elaborate full-sized rooms with or without a working railroad, as

Fig. 9-9. Jay Cain's 16' x 30' empire contains some very realistic scenery. A good track-planning tip is to leave room for buildings and scenery. In other words, don't try to cram in too much track. Photo by Andy Sperandeo.

Fig. 9-10. This large O gauge Lionel layout is a re-creation of the one built for Lionel's New York showroom in 1949. This layout was built by the Jackson (Mississippi) Society of Model Engineers. Photo by Amos McCormick.

shown in figs. 9-6 and 9-7. Collectors build glassed-in cases for rare or exceptionally clean examples. They might have sections for engines, cars, or accessories, all neatly arranged by year or model variation. Still others collect complete sets or even boxes made by Lionel early in its history.

BUILDING A BIGGER LAYOUT

As you get more and more involved in this hobby, you'll want to build a bigger layout. Often a modeler builds a series of layouts over time, each one bigger and better than the last.

That's because track-planning and model-building skills improve with practice. Some Lionel layouts fill entire basements. One example is Stan Roy's fabulous railroad, shown in fig. 9-8. Another is Jay Cain's layout, shown in fig. 9-9.

The layout that really inspired me as a youngster was the 1949 Lionel showroom layout. I hope to build one like it soon. Classic Toy Trains magazine ran a feature in its November 1993 issue on a replica of that famous layout, figs. 9-10, 9-11, and 9-12, which is part of a tourist attraction at Northpark Mall in

Jackson, Mississippi. I hope those photos inspire some of you to dream about building something like it one day.

OPERATION

Operation of your railroad to a pre-determined timetable is yet another facet of this hobby. You can organize train schedules by classification: Express passenger trains have preference over freights. Freights made up exclusively of refrigerator cars or "reefers" heading to market get the highball over just plain merchandise runs. Set up switching moves based on the industries or operating

Fig. 9-11. Another view of the Jackson Society of Model Engineers' layout. Scenes of large, well-done layouts like this one can serve as inspiration and get newcomers thinking about the dream layout they will one day build. Photo by Amos McCormick.

accessories on your pike. It's all part of the fun.

HIGH-TECH ADDITIONS

You may also want to explore the high-tech area of the hobby—electronics, automatic operation, signaling, and computer applications. With Lionel's three-rail operation, it's simple to divide a layout into blocks, which makes it easy to add a circuit that will tell you where your train is. New advances in electronics make exciting products available at reasonable cost. In the future I see Lionel trains being run by the family computer with the engineer routing trains effortlessly over hill and dale without the fear of collision. The next decade or so will be very exciting for the hobby.

LEARNING ABOUT REAL TRAINS

Many excellent books and videotapes are available on all aspects of real railroading. Learning about the prototype is enjoyable in itself, and it will help you build better models. Since you can't possibly learn everything about trains from books, you may want to take an Amtrak trip or visit a railroad museum.

People who love to watch, photograph, and learn about real trains are called railfans. This interest can be a separate hobby, and many model railroaders also consider themselves railfans.

Remember that railroads are dangerous places and are off limits to the general public for that reason. If you're going to watch trains, do so from a safe area on public property.

PHOTOGRAPHY

Taking photos of your layout can be fun. Sometimes you'll see things that need improvement in the photos that you

Fig. 9-12. In this final view of the re-created showroom layout by the Jackson Society of Model Engineers, we get to see the layout's impressive control panel. Photo by Amos McCormick.

don't see with your eyes. Photography of model railroads takes a bit of experience, but it is not that hard to master with the combination of patience and good equipment. Buying a good camera with a macro lens is the best way to start. These lenses are designed especially to take close-up or detailed photos. Most macro lenses stop down to f/32—that is, f/32 is the smallest lens opening—to give you the best in overall sharpness and greatest depth of field.

You can take good photographs either with bounce flash (off a ceiling or white card) or with a few inexpensive photofloods, available at any camera shop. Buy a book on indoor photography, focus carefully, and use a tripod and cable release for stability. And don't forget to use your imagination. That's important.

FELLOWSHIP

Finally, to expand both your knowledge and the circle of people who share your interest in trains, you can join a club in your area or national groups such as the TCA, LCCA (Lionel Collectors Club of America), LOTS (Lionel Operating Train Society), or TTOS (Toy Train Operating Society). Some folks have the best of both worlds—they belong to a modular club that can set up its layout at the TCA meets. Great! Ask at your local hobby shop if there are any Lionel clubs in the area. Or consider starting one of your own.

Those are just a few of the many possible avenues for you to explore in the months and years ahead. My hope is that after reading this book and seeing how easy and how much fun it is to build a fully operational Lionel layout, you'll be hooked on this hobby for many happy years.

Fig. 9-13. Mike Grandinetti and his family set up a beautiful 8' x 8' Lionel layout each Christmas season. Temporary layouts like this can be a lot of fun, too. Photo by Chris Becker.

Whether you build just a temporary layout for the holidays, like the one shown in fig. 9-13, or an empire laid out in the basement year round, the magic never ends. And that's the way it should be. Happy model railroading—now and in the future.

O GAUGE MODEL RAILROADING SUPPLIES

Arttista
105 Woodring Ln.
Newark, DE 19702
(metal, hand-painted O scale
figures and accessories)

Bachmann (Plasticville)
1400 E. Erie Ave.
Philadelphia, PA 19124
(snap-together building kits)

Bowser Mfg. Co., Inc.
21 Howard St., P.O. Box 322
Montoursville, PA 17754
(three-rail trolleys, O gauge
figures and detail parts)

Buildings Unlimited
P.O. Box 239K
Nazareth, PA 18064-0239
(O gauge structure kits)

CTT, Inc.
109 Medallion Center
Dallas, TX 75214
(track planning templates for
three-rail track)

Curtis Hi-Rail Products, Inc.
P.O. Box 385
North Stonington, CT 06359
(three-rail switches and track
products)

GarGraves Trackage
Corporation
Box 255-A
North Rose, NY 14516
(flexible three-rail and sectional
track with wood ties)

K-Line
MDK, Inc.
P.O. Box 2831
Chapel Hill, NC 27515
(three-rail O gauge trains and
accessories)

Lionel Trains, Inc.
50625 Richard W. Blvd.
Chesterfield, MI 48051-2493
(three-rail electric trains, track,
and accessories)

Marx Trains
209 E. Butterfield Rd.
Suite 228
Elmhurst, IL 60126
(metal, lithographed O gauge cars
and locomotives)

M.T.H. Electric Trains
7020 Columbia Gateway Dr.
Columbia, MD 21046
(Standard and O gauge locomotives, cars, track, and
accessories)

QSIndustries, Inc.
3800 SW Cedar Hills Blvd. #224
Beaverton, OR 97005
(electronic reversing units and
sound units)

Ross Custom Switches
Box 110
North Stonington, CT 06359
(three-rail switches)

Weaver Models
Box 231
Northumberland, PA 17857
(three-rail locomotives and rolling
stock)

Williams Electric Trains
8835-F Columbia 100 Parkway
Columbia, MD 21045
(three-rail locomotives and rolling
stock)

Woodland Scenics
P.O. Box 98
Linn Creek, MO 65052
(ballast and landscaping materials
for all scales)

CLUBS, ASSOCIATIONS, AND MAGAZINES
FOR LIONEL COLLECTORS AND OPERATORS

Classic Toy Trains Magazine
Kalmbach Publishing Co.
21027 Crossroads Circle
P.O. Box 1612
Waukesha, WI 53187

K-Line Collectors Club
P.O. Box 2831
Chapel Hill, NC 27515

Lionel Collectors Club of
America (LCCA)
Business Office
P.O. Box 479
LaSalle, IL 61301

Lionel Operating Train Society
(LOTS)
c/o 7408 138th Place, N.E.
Redmond, WA 98052-4008

Lionel Railroader Club
c/o Lionel Trains, Inc.
50625 Richard W. Blvd.
Chesterfield, MI 48051-2493

MTH Railroad Club
7020 Columbia Gateway Dr.
Columbia, MD 21046

Toy Train Operating Society
(TTOS)
Suite 308
25 W. Walnut Street
Pasadena, CA 91103

Train Collectors Association
P.O. Box 248
Strasburg, PA 17579